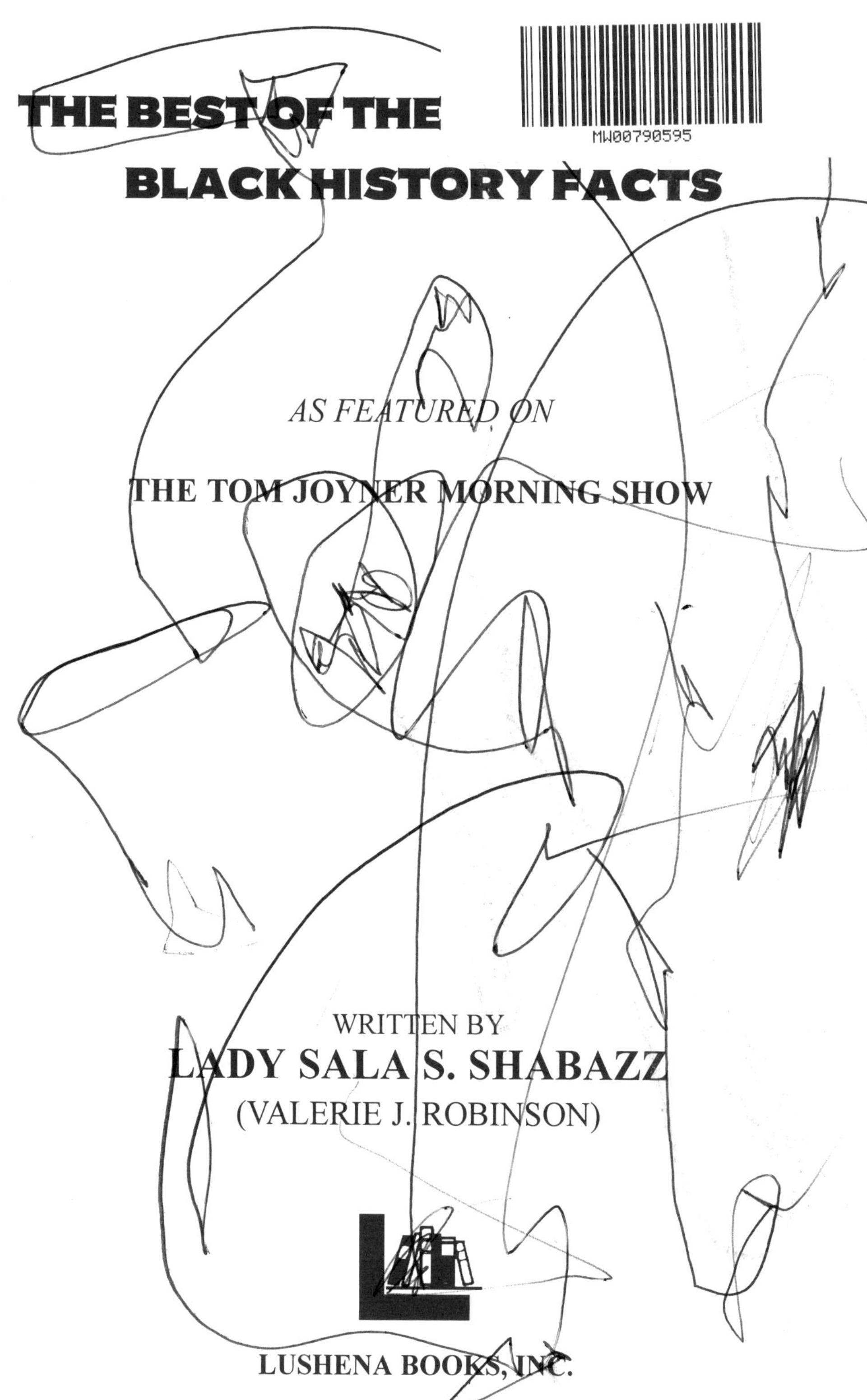

THE BEST OF THE BLACK HISTORY FACTS

AS FEATURED ON

THE TOM JOYNER MORNING SHOW

WRITTEN BY
LADY SALA S. SHABAZZ
(VALERIE J. ROBINSON)

LUSHENA BOOKS, INC.

THE BEST OF
LITTLE KNOWN BLACK HISTORY FACTS

By
LADY SALA S. SHABAZZ

First Printing: 1997
Second Printing: 1998
Third Printing: 2002

Published and Distributed by:
Lushena Books, Inc.
1804 W. Irving Park Road
Chicago, IL 60613

ISBN: 1-930097-45-X

Printed in the United States of America

TABLE OF CONTENTS

DEDICATION

THIS BOOK IS DEDICATED

TO THE MEMORY OF MY MOTHER

MATTIE G. ROBINSON

AN ANGEL

SPECIAL THANKS

TO

THE CREATOR

THE ANCESTORS OF THE SLAVE TRADE

TOM JOYNER

PREFACE

Requests for this publication have been received on the "Tom Joyner Morning Show" since early 1995, and continue to date. It is belated, for some individuals, however, still on time and contains pertinent information long sought after. Humbly specials thanks is given to:

The Creator, who makes all things possible / the Gye Nyame.

Ms. Mattie G. Robinson, my mother, who passed on May 6, 1997, encouraging and supporting every endeavor that was ever envisioned;

To the ancestors of the entrapment, kidnapping, Middle passage, slave trade, plantations of Africa, the Carribbean, Central and South America and, of course, North America and the lynchings of African people to date.

To the establishment of The Black Inventions Museum which catapulted the idea of writing this information in a simplified form;

To Janie Chavers, sister/friend, for consistently being there and encouraging me when things were trying;

To Dr. Patricia Bath, Scientist/Inventor for relentless support and her strength and perseverance in her quest to prevent blindness in people of color in underserved communities;

To Vonda Marshall, Esq. for friendship incorporated with legal expertise and guidance;

To my mentor, Irving Clark, for leadership and inspiration;

To Ade Singleton, whose spiritual enlightenment assisted in maintaining a sense of sanity;

To Elaine Padilla, for secretarial and editing skills that are only surpassed by a longlasting friendship.

To Tom Joyner, for his vision of including inspirational historical information on the Tom Joyner Morning Show and without whom these facts would not be aired and this publication possibly would not have taken place;

To Lador Frank, staff of the Tom Joyner Morning Show, for encouragement in the pursuit of printing this publication;

To the numerous researchers, authors and writers of publications and dessiminators of information listed in the bibliography, in particular: McKinley Burt, Jr., Chandler White Publishing Company, Lerone Bennett, Jr., Anthony T. Browder, Middleton Harris, Johnson Publishing Co., Joan Potter with Constance Claytor, Janus Adams;

To the Masters of the Education of African people - Henry E. Baker, Carter G. Woodson, J.A. Rogers, Dr. Yosef ben-Jochannan, John Henri Clarke, Dr. Leonard Jeffries, Ivan Van Sertima, and Frances Cress Weisling whose footsteps I humbly attempt to follow;

To IMAHKUS Nzingah Okofu, Nana Okofu Iture Kwakui of One Africa Productions Ghana, West Africa, for their spiritual devotion as keepers of the Door of No Return at Cape Coast;

To my adopted son, Hamza Salifu (Fehe Jua Wubontuo) for his sincere love for African unity throughout the world.

To Rabbi Kohain and Mrs. Mable HaLevi, for nourishment of the spirit and body in all my Sankofa journeys;

To Michael Young of Medasi Incorporated for providing the second Sankofa experience.

To the printer, Pat and Curtis Gatlin of Matson Printing Corp., an African American printing company, who exemplifies the best in the community; and, to

All those who have encouraged the endeavors of the presentation of "Little Known Black History Facts" that highlight African people accomplishments in all areas of our existence.

To all those individuals attending the display of The Black Inventions Museum in various cities; and, listeners of the Tom Joyner Morning Show who have encouraged, contributed and supported the endeavors of presenting the "Little Known Black History Facts" that highlight accomplishments of African people in all areas of our existence.

ASANTE SANA! MEDASI!

FORWARD

This history book begins each segment with graphic visual symbols of the Akan people of Ghana. Visual symbols like Black history continually reveal truths and hidden knowledge. Where bondage, ignorance and arrogance exist truths have to be discerned. This book attempts to demystify many stereotypes of a people. The author aptly gives concise data, condensed as a skillfully compact visual symbol. We think in pictures or graphics.

This world will never assume its rightful balance, its normal peace, harmony and racial richness in composition until Black peoples are in their rightful place. All peoples have been adversely affected by racism but none have a history comparable to Black peoples. Our riches have nurtured and sustained others often at our own expense. You cannot rape a parent and maintain psycho-sociological, political equilibrium. Science has revealed the planetary mother. Her name was Denkenash "Lucy," she lived about 3-1/2 million years ago in East Africa. Many sciences agree on the origins of humankind: 1) archaeology - fossils 2) genetics - mitachondria DNA 3) linguistics 4) prehistoric art and ruins. The Bible confirms the African Edenic truth "God made them all of one blood." Our Genesis mother travelled, Her discendants migrated to all the continents including Mesopotamia. Along with the major contributions of Black men, author Lady Sala S. Shabazz includes the heroic saga of women who continued the paradigm of Denkenash, from Queen Hathshepsut to Queen Calafia, California, the Black Kali. The author Lady Sala reports on the extraordinary geniusness of men, from Imhotep, Nat Turner, Benjamin Banneker and more.

The first Akan symbol presented in this book restates the Genesis truth, a symbol entitled Gye Nyame. Gye Nyame represents God Supreme. It was our faith in the Supreme Creator that caused our multiplication, our ability to overcome against the odds, our ability to build great civilizations and rich culture, our ability to walk humbly with our God. Gye Nyame in glyph form is the twice broken circle, the globe with whirlwind, vortex of super-conduction. The Akan is axiomatic speech say "If you want to tell it to God then tell it to the wind." The people of Kemet called this the "unknown God" meaning so vast and powerful God cannot be confined. God is like the whirlwind seen by Ezekiel in which he saw a lion, an ox/bull, an eagle and man, principalities, attributes, powers and personifications. Gye Nyame is like the whirlwind that came on the day of penticost, split tongues of fire, substance and life. The very foundations of world culture can be better understood by the inclusion Black history and culture into your life's curriculum. This book attempts to present facts to help you read between the lines in order to discern the truth.

There are two other Akan symbols in this book which are of particular importance to Blacks in the New World, the Americas. Nkyinkyimie the twisting and turning pattern, and also Sankofa, meaning turn back and fetch it, both of these graphic symbols are about assimilation, change, adaptation, overcoming endurance. African Americans have sung "We shall overcome" but now must sing "We have overcome." From a more sure understanding of history, we must actively affect the global future. Students should memorize the facts of this book, and deliberately change the future. The mental puzzles and mazes of Nkyinkyimie are meant to reinvent, to analyze, synthesize and act. Sankofa is represented in both graphic and three dimensional glyphs. The graphic pattern is composed of two spirals that twirl in opposite directions. The Sankofa picturegram in three dimensions is a bird which stands on a step pyramid and looks back over its wing and tail from when it had come. Sankofa incorporates two parables 1) regrets are in vain. 2) turn back and fetch it. The metaphor is regression as in psychology, one must know your personal psychic individual history in order for well being. Turn back and fetch it, is also the collective history, your family, ethnic group, clan, race, national and global. This book is about research and history which effect both individual psychic mind-set and also the national legacy and Black global perspectives. Regrets means you must be wise in the face of knowledge. Too much anger over periods of time will corrode the soul. Violence has its place but must not overflow its bounds. This aspect of Sankofa in Kemet was axiomatically expressed, "Do not eat thy heart." The truth of Sankofa was written on the temple walls of Kemet and copied by foreigners and ascribed to the Greeks. The famous saying on temple walls was "Man Know Thyself." Read, meditate, discern, know yourself, your human self, your family self and your God self.

Rosalind Jeffries, Ph.D.

HISTORY

Napoleon has been quoted as once saying, "What is history? History is nothing but a lie agreed upon!"

This is an indication of what has happened when recording the Story of the African, at home and abroad. Therefore, it is imperative that African people record and circulate the information in all mediums, through books, magazines, circulars, and yes, now, internet/cyberspace. However, in these areas of communication, it is reminded that information concerning the African diaspora maintain accuracy and authenticity.

The facts are clear. For several decades publications by the established academia have been bias about the truth of the contributions, accomplishments and history of the African experience. Constant challenges, doubts and cover-ups continue to persist.

As defined in Webster's dictionary, "history" **1.** the branch of knowledge dealing with past events. **2.** a continuous, systematic narrative of past events as relating to a particular people, country, period, person, etc., usually written in chronological order. **3.** the aggregate of past events. **4.** the record of past events, esp. in connection with the human race. **5.** a past that is full of important, unusual, or interesting events. **6.** acts, ideas, or events that will or can shape the course of the future. **7.** a systematic account of any set of natural phenomena, without reference to time. **8.** a drama representing historical events."

Fortunately, for the African diaspora, independent researchers and scholars, such as J.A. Rogers, Henry E. Baker, Dr. Yosef ben-Jochannan, John Henri Clarke, Ivan Van Sertima, Anthony T. Browder, Professor Leonard Jeffries, Dr. Rosalind Jeffries, and many others, have accepted the mission of writing numerous publications that contain documented, authenticated and unquestionable proof of the existence of the African before other nationalities evolved.

The information contained in "The Best of the Little Known History Facts" as presented on the "Tom Joyner Morning Show" is from the various publications and periodicals as outlined in the References and Bibliography. Read, read, read.

INTRODUCTION

LADY SALA S. SHABAZZ is the founder and curator of THE BLACK INVENTIONS MUSEUM, INC., a Non-Profit Public Benefit Corporation. The Black Inventions Musuem was established as a mobile display of Black Inventors and Inventions, scientific and industrial, which enhance our lives on a daily basis.

In 1988, as an independent book publisher, Sala Enterprises, and author of children's books, i.e. **The Kwanzaa Coloring Book, Flags of the African People, Kwanzaa - An African Celebration** and **The Cinco de Mayo Coloring Book**; and as a vendor at various cultural events, LADY SALA began selling a poster entitled "Black Inventions Live On", published by Chandler White Publishing Company in Illinois. At that time, the idea came to LADY SALA to create and sell a miniature inventions museum highlighting inventions by Black inventors. After researching the cost of miniatures, and finding the expenses prohibitive, LADY SALA took items from her home, put them in a box and began gathering additional information and documentation on inventions and inventors.

In February, 1991, the first display of the Museum was presented for a Jack & Jill Group in Yorba Linda, California with only two tables of inventions. However, continued research and inventions were collected. In 1992, the Gardena African American-Cultural Arts Foundation invited LADY SALA to present The Black Inventions Museum for their Black History Month program on February 29, 1992. During the course of the day, an inventor saw the Museum, and after several meetings encouraged LADY SALA to contact an interested party who could financially assist in the Museum's presentation. LADY SALA met with ICE CUBE, the well-known rapper, movie star, director, and Patricia Charbonnet, his manager in June 1992.

In July 1992, ICE CUBE and STREET KNOWLEDGE FOUNDATION endorsed, and THE McKENZIE RIVER PARTNERSHIP sponsored, The Black Inventions Museum with a sizable financial donation for the Museum's presentation at the African Marketplace and Cultural Faire, a City of Los Angeles event. During the last weekend of the African Marketplace, Everett Staton, Corporate Sales Executive of Black Expo USA, witnessed the phenomena of the response to the Museum's presentation, and after negotiations invited SALA ENTERPRISES and THE BLACK INVENTIONS MUSEUM to participate and become a part of the 14 city tour of Black Expo USA in 1993. After a successful tour, Black Expo USA requested that The BLACK INVENTIONS MUSEUM participate in the 15 city tour in 1994, and subsequent years, 1995 and 1996.

LADY SALA, incorporated The Black Inventions Museum in 1994 as a Non-Profit Public Benefit Corporation, and directed the participation in various schools, colleges, cultural groups, churches, corporations, organizations, festivals and conferences, both national and international (totals over 26 states, 160 cities, and included the countries of Bahia, Brazil, South America; Toronto, Canada; and, Ghana, West Africa).

LADY SALA's dedication to the promotion of positive images and self-esteem are exemplified in her endeavors of research, investigation and documentation of the magnificent contributions of African people throughout the world. In addition, networking assistance is provided to individuals who have communicated with her nationwide to assist them in the development of their ideas and innovations.

On September 15, 1994, while presenting THE BLACK INVENTIONS MUSEUM at the Annual 25th Congressional Black Caucus, held in Washington, D.C., LADY SALA, was approached by TOM JOYNER of the TOM JOYNER MORNING SHOW, requesting her to write and provide the show with the "Unknown History Facts". By October, 1994 the first submission was presented to Tom Joyner, and subsequently, the name changed to the "Little Known Black History Facts". Listeners of the Tom Joyner Morning Show telephoned weekly requesting a book that contained the information as aired. Encouraged by the request, LADY SALA, began formulating and gathering the best of the facts as featured in this publication. The reader should note that the facts contained herein are only a fraction of the facts which are all considered "the best" making these selections difficult to choose.

In 1996 LADY SALA traveled to Ghana, West Africa for the first time. This trip spiritually spearheaded The Black Inventions Museum's first overwhelmingly successful debut to Ghana during African History Month in March, 1997, displaying the Museum at the W.E.B. DuBois Pan African Center, the University of Cape Coast, the University of Legon and the University of Science and Technology. In August, 1997, with its "Little Known Black History Facts", The Black Inventions Museum stimulated the minds of everyone who was privileged to see the Museum at PANAFEST in Cape Coast, Ghana.

LADY SALA S. SHABAZZ, continues to read, inquire, and receive information from various sources, including listeners of the Tom Joyner Morning Show, with facts and information that are unknown. Documented information is welcomed from individuals and/or any source who seek to enhance and supplement the education of society. Thus, providing information to people of all nationalities with simple facts that stimulate a renewed respect for the significant inventions, innovations and historical contributions of people of African heritage.

The "Little Known Black History Facts", as featured on the Tom Joyner Morning Show, is compiled, condensed information by various researchers, authors, newspaper reporters as indicated in the bibliography contained herein. These individuals have eloquently contributed in greater detail to the database of information as presented on the Tom Joyner Morning Show. Further reading of these materials is encouraged, suggested, and imperative.

In the near future, a comprehensive publication of the "Little Known Black History Facts" as featured on the "Tom Joyner Morning Show" will be available.

GYE NYAME

ONLY GOD

MEANING:

THE SYMBOL DEPICTS THE BELIEF IN THE SUPREMACY OF GOD AND SIGNIFIES GOD'S OMNIPOTENCE, OMNIPRESENCE AND OMNISCIENCE.

GOD
HAS POWER OVER
EVERYTHING AND EVERYONE.

THE ASHANTI
AND THE SIGNIFICANCE OF GOLD

The Ashanti of Ghana, West Africa, were well known for their wealth in gold as well as the craftsmanship of their goldsmiths. The objects created by Africa's goldsmiths first drew admiration, then envy from the early Europeans. For the Ashanti, gold was a public display of status, wealth and independence and among the Ashanti, the right to wear it was determined by the Asantehene or King. Supreme status in the Ashanti's society was measured by the weight of gold, the intricacy of the designs and the richness of their kente cloth. Records show that long before the Portuguese opened up the West African "Gold Coast" to the Europeans, there was a flourishing trade between the Ashanti and Arab traders of Northern Africa. Little survives of the masses of gold dust, gold beads, necklaces, hair ornaments, rings and bracelets taken by the Portuguese during the four centuries of trade. The British also demanded the sacred golden stool (which they never obtained) fought and took gold from the Capital City of Kumasi, Ghana in the year 1900. Bodies have been adorned with gold for centuries. Until recently, men used to outdo the women in the number of gold pieces they wore. The Entertainers of today with the chains, necklaces and rings are only re-enacting and reconnecting with their ancestral past.

SANKOFA

SYMBOLIZES: *RETURN AND PICK IT UP. LEARN FROM THE PAST. PICK UP THE GEMS OF THE PAST. A CONSTANT REMINDER THAT THE PAST IS NOT ALL SHAMEFUL AND THAT THE FUTURE MAY BE PROFITABLY BUILT ON ASPECTS OF THE PAST.*

CHAPTER ONE

1. THE OLDEST MEDICAL TEXTBOOKS
2. IMHOTEP
3. THE ORIGIN OF CHESS
4. THE ORIGIN OF ZODIAC AND THE MEANING OF "HOROSCOPE"
5. NILE VALLEY ORIGIN OF THE GREAT SEAL OF THE UNITED STATES - DOLLAR BILL
6. SHIPBUILDING-AN AFRICAN TRADITION
7. TIMBUKTU - THE FIRST UNIVERSITY
8. THE BURNING OF INCENSE

THE OLDEST MEDICAL TEXTBOOKS - THE EDWIN SMITH PAPYRUS AND EBERS PAPYRUS OF EGYPT

The Edwin Smith Papyrus is the oldest medical textbook in existence believed to be written in the 18th Dynasty or 1550 B.C.E. (Before the Christian Era) and considered to be a copy of the original document created in the first dynasty. The ancient physicians and priests of the Nile Valley were instructed in Temples called the "HOUSE OF LIFE". The Edwin Smith Papyrus was published in 1930 and describes 48 different injuries to the head, face, neck, thorax and spinal column and the appropriate surgical methods for treating them. There are more than 90 anatomical terms and the use of the word "Brain" and references to the neurological relationship between the spinal cord and the nervous system and the body.

The medical journal known as the Ebers Papyrus dates back to 1500 B.C.E. contains a broad range of medical science and includes chapters on the pulse and cardiovascular system, dermatology, dentistry, gynecology, opthalmology, obstetrics, tumors, burns, fractures, intestinal disorders and much more. There is evidence that the physicians of Egypt practiced circumcision, brain surgery and were extremely knowledgeable in gynecology and obstetrics.

The oldest medical textbooks - found in Egypt, which is and has always been a country in Africa.

IMHOTEP
TRUE FATHER OF MEDICINE

IMHOTEP was a Black Egyptian who lived about 2,980 B.C., where he established a reputation as a healer. As King Zoser's Chief physician, he was also a Scribe, Priest, Architect, Astronomer, Magician, Poet and Physician. A best known saying of his is: "EAT, DRINK AND BE MERRY FOR TOMORROW WE SHALL DIE".

Evidence has proven that Egyptians diagnosed and treated more than 200 diseases. They knew how to detect diseases by the shape, color, or condition of the external parts of the body such as skin, nails, tongue, hair, etc. They practiced surgery and extracted medicine from plants.

Imhotep knew of the circulation of the blood, which is 4000 years before it was known in Europe!

The Egyptian men were more skilled in medicine than any other, therefore, the Greeks sent their young men to be educated in Egypt. When the Egyptian civilization crossed the Mediterranean Sea to become the foundation of the Greek Culture, the great teachings of Imhotep were absorbed there. But since the Greeks were seriously involved in creating the illusion that they were the originators of everything, Imhotep was forgotten for thousands of years and Hippocrates, a legendary Greek, who lived 2000 YEARS after Imhotep became known as the "Father of Medicine".

THE ORIGIN OF THE GAME OF CHESS

Man has created and enjoyed strategic board games since the beginning of civilization. There is a Bas-Relief from the Tomb of the Ancient Egyptian Queen Nefertari playing a form of chess over 4,000 years ago. Also the story is told of a Songhay General in the intellectual centers in Timbuktu who bungled a military campaign and explained that he became so engrossed in a chess game that he paid no attention to the reports of his scouts.

Chess was introduced into Europe between 700 and 900 A.D. by the Muslims and by both the Moors in Spain and Saracen Traders in Italy. It steadily increased in popularity in spite of some initial opposition from the church which considered chess a gambling game, and therefore sinful.

Medieval European chess was played by the same rules as its Muslim counterpart SHATRANJ until the second half of the Fifteenth Century. Then certain innovations such as increasing the powers of the Queen and Bishop were devised to accelerate the tempo of the game and by the middle of the Sixteenth Century the basic rules for playing chess as we know it today had become standard.

The origin of chess - from Africa.

THE ORIGIN OF THE ZODIAC AND THE MEANING OF THE WORD HOROSCOPE

The study of the heavens and the mapping of the stars is an age-old science which takes centuries of observation and analysis. The people of Ancient Egypt, also known as Kemet, who were the early inhabitants of the Nile Valley, identified groups of stars stretched across the sky, and whose rising followed each other by a period of ten days. The division of the Kemetic year into 36 weeks of ten days each meant that each week was ruled over by a specific constellation.

Determined thousands of years ago, this is the process that a circle would consist of 360 degrees. The people of Kemet further divided the heavens into 12 divisions each in the Southern, Northern and Central skies. These 36 divisions were then divided among the three seasons which emerged the 12 signs of the Zodiac. The stars were associated with various gods and were called decans. Each zodiacal sign was associated with a decan who was referred to as one of the Watchers of the Hours and regarded as messengers of the greater gods or of the god Horus himself, which is the origin of the word horoscope. Each zodiac sign was purely symbolic, and represented the relationship between the appearance of certain stars overhead and specific activity taking place on earth below.

The original and first Zodiac chart was located in the ceiling of an observatory in the Temple of Dendera. It was "discovered" by Napoleon's troops in 1799 and dynamited from the ceiling. After a series of owners, it was sold to Louis XVIII for 150,000 Francs and is now located in the Louvre Museum, Paris, France. The Zodiac's origin is AFRICAN.

NILE VALLEY ORIGIN OF THE GREAT SEAL OF THE UNITED STATES AND THE DOLLAR BILL

The first of Great Seals appeared in the 7th Century Europe and were used exclusively by royalty to make a distinction between the lesser seals which were used for personal or business affairs. Over the years, great seals have come to represent the heart and soul of a nation.

The United States decided to create a great seal and incorporated into its design elements of masonry, numerology and Egyptian symbolism. After several committees were formed beginning July 4, 1776, the third and final committee met on May 4, 1782 and finalized the designs which are on both sides of the official great seal. Slight modifications were made of the front of the Great Seal in 1885 and the emblem has remained unchanged since.

By 1933 Roosevelt was so impressed with the correlation of the Latin Phrase "Novus Ordo Seclorum" and his presidential theme "New Deal" that he decided to use both sides of the Great Seal on the Dollar Bill instead of a coin.

The pyramid and the eye above it which represents the eye of Heru-the Son of God establishes the Egyptian link on the reverse side of the Great Seal. The front side of the seal is similar to the Nile Valley Image of Heru, and the differences represents the cultural nuances which were unique to the United States. Above the eagle's head are 13 stars which are arranged in the form of the Magen David, which is also called the Seal of Solomon. This is an ancient symbol that predates Judaism and represents two pyramids. The two pyramids symbolize the two pillars of Solomon, which play a role in ritualistic masonry. The Dollar Bill - its symbols originating from Egypt.

SHIPBUILDING
AN AFRICAN TRADITION

Egypt's history records that the ability of the African People of Kemet, Nubia and Ethiopia to explore new worlds, transport goods and ferry huge stones for temple constructions was due to their capacity to build and navigate a variety of seagoing vessels. Papyrus reed boats had been in use in the Nile Valley since the earliest dynasties and the development of navigational skills allowed for the building of larger ships and travel. The first use of a sail on a ship has also been traced to the Nile Valley in Egypt.

In 1970 a Norwegian born ethnologist Thor Heyerdahl and a crew of seven sailed a Papyrus Reed boat named RA-II from the West Coast of Africa to the Caribbean proving that African sailors in similar boats sailed across the Atlantic Ocean to the "New World". He based the design of the boat on paintings found in Nile Valley monuments and he hired Africans to construct the ship.

The most impressive ancient ship ever discovered was the 4,600 year old barge found buried near the Great Pyramid of Khufu at Giza in 1954. And in the fall of 1991, Egyptologists discovered a fleet of 12 royal ships which were found at Abydos in an ancient burial ground 280 miles south of Cairo. These ships are 50 to 60 feet long and are estimated to be about 5,000 years old and believed to be the earliest boats found on earth. Shipbuilding - an African Tradition.

TIMBUKTU
THE FIRST UNIVERSITY

Numerous jokes or expressions using the word "TIMBUKTU" have been made without knowing what TIMBUKTU is. History has recorded Timbuktu as a great learning center and ideal market. The CITY OF TIMBUKTU, located in Mali, Africa, in the year 1526 was a bustling city which grew out of an oasis. During that time it was a good location where camel caravans from North Africa and ships from the West would meet to trade. As an ideal market and trade center, items such as gold, metal working, pottery, cloth manufacture, silk, jewelry, books, firearms and food items such as smoked fish, rice, fruit, onions, honey, tobacco, spices, tea and coffee were bought and sold. Industries were developed such as the manufacture of boots, slippers, book bindings and crafted leather goods.

Not only as a center of Islam and the location of the University of Sankore, but it was a city where scholars from around the world would come and study not only the religion of Islam, but physicians performed surgeries such as the removal of cataracts from the eye. It also produced judges and scholars and priests. To this day TIMBUKTU still functions as a market and trading city. TIMBUKTU was no joke and should be remembered as a learning center with universities, hospitals and the ideal trade market of West Africa.

THE BURNING OF INCENSE AN AFRICAN TRADITION

Among the Egyptians of all periods of the time table, one of the most important ceremonies was the burning of incense. Each substance used in the composition of incense was supposed to possess magical properties and the smell produced by burning them together was believed to be much liked by the gods.

The smoke was thought to form a material vehicle on which the words of the prayers recited by the worshipper would mount up to heaven and then they reached the divine being to whom they were addressed, the odor of the incense which accompanied the prayers caused the divine being to receive them graciously, and to grant the supplicant their prayer.

It is also written that the soul of the dead person ascended into heaven by means of the incense which was burnt on the person's behalf. The burning of incense - an ancient African custom.

SANKOFA

"A climate of alienation has a profound effect on the Black personality, particularly on the educated Black, who has the opportunity to see how the rest of the world regards him and his people. It often happens that the black intellectual thus loses confidence in his own potential and that of his race. Often the effect is so crushing that some Blacks, having evidence to the contrary, still find it hard to accept the fact that we really were the first to civilize the world."

—Cheikh Anta Diop

BESA SAKA

SYMBOLIZES AFFLUENCE AND POWER

CHAPTER TWO

1. QUEEN HATHSHEPSUT
2. CLEOPATRA
3. QUEEN YAA ASANTEWA
4. QUEEN NZINGHA
5. QUEEN OF SHEBA
6. QUEEN SOPHIA CHARLOTTE
7. QUEEN CALAFIA

QUEEN HATSHEPSUT - THE PHARAOH / THE WARRIOR

Queen Hatshepsut (Hat-shep-soot), is the story of a Queen-Mother who stole the throne from a child-pharaoh in a coup d'etat and went on to proclaim herself as Pharaoh. She ruled Egypt for twenty-one years until the child-pharaoh Tuthmosis grew to adulthood and destroyed her.

As a princess Hathsepsut became chief aide to her king father who was stricken with paralysis. With her father she managed state matters and became co-ruler of Egypt. Before her father passed, he married Hathsepsut to her half-brother in order that she would become Queen. In her early twenties, wanting more power, she dressed herself in the most sacred of the Pharaoh's official costumes, and with the royal scepter in one hand and the sacred crook in the other, she mounted the throne and proclaimed herself Pharaoh of Egypt, and became the first and the greatest female ruler of all time.

During her 21 year reign her accomplishments were in trade, art and architecture. To immortalize herself, she ordered two obelisks to be quarried. The quarrying, transporting and erecting of these 100 foot needle-like structures represented remarkable achievements in engineering and the control she exercised over Egypt's resources of manpower, equipment and materials.

It is recorded that Hathsepsut personally led several military campaigns during her reign. Her end came prematurely and mysteriously, and some historians say that Tuthmosis II seized the throne and killed her. Her reign was one of the most outstanding in the 18th Dynasty of Egypt, proving that a woman can be a strong and effective ruler.

QUEEN OF SHEBA - WHO'S THAT LADY

The legendary Queen of Sheba - had various names at different periods of time but two of the most interesting were to the Ancient Greeks, she was the Black Minerva and to King Solomon of Israel, she was the Queen of Sheba. To her own people, she was known as Makeda, The Beautiful - the Queen of both Ethiopia and Saba in Southern Arabia. Beautiful and very rich, she had heard a great deal about the wealth of Israel and the wisdom of King Solomon. Makeda decided to travel to Jerusalem with a caravan of almost 800 camels and mules which were loaded with precious stones, metals and other valuable items.

During her six month visit, she was impressed with King Solomon and gave up her religion and promised him that if she had a male child, she would crown him King of Ethiopia. This was very significant since her country had always been ruled by women. When Makeda decided to return to Ethiopia, King Solomon gave her a ring to identify if she had a male child from their romance. Exactly nine months and five days after she left King Solomon she gave birth to a male child and named him Menelik, who was "the son of the Wise Man".

Menelik at the age of 22 traveled to Jerusalem to meet his father and when he arrived people already knew that he was the son of King Solomon, and when Solomon saw him he embraced his son and promised him the Kingdom of Israel. Menelik had promised Makeda that he would return to Ethiopia, Solomon then anointed Menelik King of Ethiopia and gave him the name of David. Makeda, the Queen of Sheba descendants ruled Ethiopia until the death of Haile Selassie in the 1960s. The Queen of Sheba - she was one the most beautiful and richest African Woman rulers in East African history and culture.

QUEEN YAA ASANTEWA
(Yah Ah-san'-te-wah)

PROTECTOR OF THE GOLDEN STOOL

Yaa Asantewa, Queen-Mother of the Ashanti State of Ejisu, spearheaded the war in 1900 between the British and the Ashanti that was named after her in an effort to protect the Golden Stool. The Golden Stool was considered a masterpiece of African Art. It was carved out of a solid block of teak and studded with golden nails and ornaments. The Golden Stool represented wealth, courage, health and strength and was to the Ashanti equivalent to the ark of the covenant. At ceremonies it was carried ahead of the King, and housed in a special building and guarded by two chiefs.

Since the late 1800s the British tried continuously to press the Ashanti to accept British rule. Ashanti Ruler Prempehi was considered the center of resistance, and eventually forced into exile. The British thought that once the sacred stool was in their possession, they could control the Ashanti Nation.

Queen Yaa Asantewa considered the demand for the Golden Stool an insult. She swore on the great oath of the Ashanti and called upon the support of her people to fight the British. The war was bloody and in 1901 the Ashanti were finally defeated. Although the Ashanti lost the war and Yaa Asantewa was captured and sent into exile, the Golden Stool was never seized.

Queen Yaa Asantewa is remembered for her brave attempt to save her nation from further indignities of the British.

QUEEN NZINGHA - THE RESISTOR

Queen Nzingha was born in 1583 in the country now known as Angola, belonging to an ethnic group called the Jagas. The Jagas were an extremely militant group who formed a human shield against the Portuguese slave traders. Nzingha never accepted the Portuguese conquest and always was on the military offensive. She formed an alliance with the Dutch, as well as many kings and heads of families, in an effort to defeat the Portuguese.

A visionary political leader, competent, self-sacrificing and devoted to the resistance movement, Nzingha, at the age of 41 became Queen of Ndongo, but preferred to be called King when leading her army in battle, dressed in men's clothing. Her most successful weapon was her personality, where she possessed masculine hardness but feminine charm, which she used depending on the need and occasion and her leadership was never seriously challenged.

In 1645 when her sister, Fungi was taken as a prisoner of war and murdered, she questioned her religious beliefs and joined the Christian religion to fight for the freedom of her country. In 1659 by the age of more than 75 years old, she had resisted the Portuguese most of her adult life. Queen Nzingha died on December 17, 1663. This great African Woman - a freedom fighter and resistor of slavery of her people.

CLEOPATRA - THE AFRICAN WOMAN

Cleopatra - an African woman was born in 69 B.C. and shared the throne with her brother when she was 18 years old. Egypt had been taken over by Rome, and Cleopatra aligned herself with Julius Caesar to reinforce her power in Egypt. Their political and romantic relationship was in an effort to save Egypt from Roman domination.

At the age of 20 when Julius Caesar was assassinated, she began a politically motivated romance with Mark Anthony. Mark Anthony became a traitor to his own people when he attempted to assist Cleopatra in her effort to save her country. Because of his love for Cleopatra, Mark Anthony was assassinated which left Cleopatra without a protector or champion for her cause to prevent her country from being ruled by Rome.

Now losing total control of her country Cleopatra then committed suicide because of her devotion and great love for Egypt, her country. Cleopatra, a shrewd politician and Egyptian nationalist - an African Woman.

QUEEN SOPHIA CHARLOTTE - THE AFRICAN QUEEN OF ENGLAND

Sophia Charlotte of North Germany became Queen of England following her marriage to King George III in 1761. Born of African heritage, she was of royalty, the second branch of the house of Mechlenburg, for which Dukes were made Governors. Her father, Charles Lewis, was to succeed as the third Duke, but unfortunately died and Sophia's Uncle became the reigning Duke. As Queen, she ruled over Great Britain, Ireland and America.

Her African features were most truly shown by the Black Artist Allan Ramsey, who painted over forty sketches of Queen Charlotte. During their marriage, King George and Queen Charlotte had 15 children. Their daughter Alexandria Victoria became the famous Queen Victoria.

As a woman of African heritage, it is interesting that Charlottetown, in Canada and Charlotte, North Carolina were both named in honor of the Black Queen of England.

THE ORIGIN OF THE NAME "CALIFORNIA" - QUEEN CALAFIA

The word California is packed with the images of "California Girls" to "California Cooler", carefree easy life, filled with pleasant weather and scenic landscapes and a never-ending frontier. The original meaning and story behind the naming of California is not taught in public schools. However, historians have recorded the following.

California is named after a nation ruled by Black Women. In 1510, the spanish writer Garcia Ordonez Montalvo wrote of an island inhabited by Black Women in which the only mineral was gold. Its ruler Queen Calafia, was not a docile heathen ruler waiting to be conquered by European explorers. She was a fierce warrior who led a nation of self-reliant women who trained huge birds called griffins to eat any man because men were only used for breeding, and only girls were kept alive. Seeking new worlds to conquer Queen Calafia set sail in a vast fleet with 500 griffins to take on the Christians seeking to hold Constantinople. There she joined two ottoman sheiks in an attack on the city. After losing several battles the Sultan and Queen were taken prisoners.

A love affair took place between Queen Calafia and the son of a European King, Talanque. After being converted to Christianity, Queen Calafia and her warrior sister Liota married two knights and set sail to fight in many battles and gained many kingdoms. Queen Calafia is the origin of the name - California.

NKYINKYIMIE

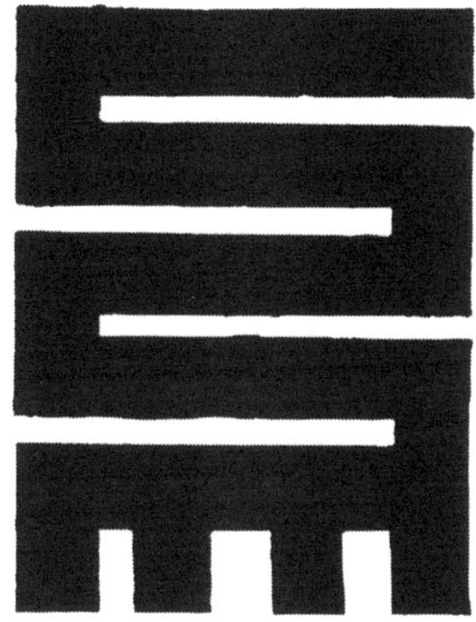

SYMBOLIZES: ***TOUGHNESS AND SELFLESS DEVOTION TO SERVICE AND THE ABILITY TO WITHSTAND DIFFICULTIES***

CHAPTER THREE

1. DENMARK VESEY
2. NAT TURNER
3. JOSEPH CINQUE
4. TOUSSAINT LE'OVERTURE
5. HARRIET TUBMAN
6. MARY JOHNSON AND HER SON WILLIAM
7. CLARA BROWN
8. UNCLE TOM - REV. JOSIAH HENSON

DENMARK VESEY - HELPING MY BROTHER MAN

Denmark Vesey was born in 1767 in Charleston, South Carolina into slavery to Captain Vesey, and sailed for 20 years with Captain Vesey to the Virgin Islands and Haiti. After winning a lottery of $1,500 he purchased his freedom for $600 and accumulated even more money and risked his lifestyle and everything to free other slaves.

Vesey became a minister of a Methodist Church in Charleston and began to recruit supporters for his planned slave revolt in Charleston. With the revolt set to go into operation on the second Sunday in July 1822, Vesey's plan was revealed by a slave who alerted white authorities.

Reacting quickly, hundreds of Black people were rounded up, including Vesey who was captured after a two day search. Never denying his intent to free his people during the trial, Vesey was hanged on July 2, 1822.

NAT TURNER
FREEDOM IS MINE

Nat Turner who was born in 1800, grew into maturity believing strongly that he was destined to lead a revolt to free his people from the harsh and cruel life of slavery. Through his constant prayer and reading of the bible, Turner believed God wanted him to conquer South Hampton County, Virginia.

On August 22, 1831 with six slaves the revolt began with Turner killing his master, Joseph Travis and his entire family. Striking nearby isolated white homes, within 48 hours the handful of followers had grown to some 60 armed and angry men. Within the county, Turner and his men killed 55 whites before deciding to turn their attack towards the county seat of Jerusalem, Virginia.

While enroute the group was overtaken by a posse and dispersed with Turner fleeing into the swamps. After eluding authorities for six weeks, Turner was captured on October 30, 1831. Given a trial, he and 16 members of his group were convicted and sentenced to death by hanging. The execution took place on November 11, 1831 in Jerusalem, Virginia.

"I would never be of service to
anyone as a slave"
-Nat Turner

JOSEPH CINQUE
BELIEVER IN SETTING YOURSELF FREE

Joseph Cinque, was born in Africa, was captured and sold into slavery in Havana, Cuba in 1839. Purchased by the Spaniards, he was placed aboard the ship, Amistad, which was preparing to set sail for Puerto Principe. Caught in a violent storm, Cinque noticed how tired the crew were becoming from their efforts in trying to keep the ship afloat. He alerted other slaves of his plan of a mutiny. Waiting for just the right moment, Cinque led the other slaves in a surprise attack. During the siege, the slaves killed all but two men, whose lives were spared so that they could navigate the ship back to Africa.

Lacking navigational knowledge, Cinque and his men did not realize that the captives were sailing the Amistad North instead of East. Sighted off Long Island, the ship was taken to port in Connecticut, where Cinque and his men were imprisoned. With the support from abolitionists, Cinque was released and went on a lecture tour to raise funds for his judicial appeals.

On March 9, 1841, with the representation of Quincy Adams, the Supreme Court ruled that Cinque and his men be set free. Afterwards, Cinque returned home to Africa.

TOUSSAINT L'OUVERTURE FIRST AFRICAN LEADER IN THE WEST

Toussaint L'Ouverture, under the guidance of his mother and Godfather who taught him French, Latin, Geometry and instilled in him a deep faith in God, was responsible for Haiti becoming an independent nation in the Americas in 1804, second to the United States. In 1791 after the Haitian revolution began with a courageous slave named Boukman, Toussaint used his skills to conquer the former French and Spanish slaveowners, defeated the British army and conquered Napoleon in Haiti and caused his defeat in Europe as well.

In 1802 when Napoleon tried to re-enslave Black people on the island of Haiti, it was Toussaint's genius that destroyed army after army and weakened Napoleon's position in France. Deceived by diplomats in an effort to make peace, he was kidnapped and taken to France and imprisoned by Napoleon until his death on April 7, 1803.

According to the research of J.A. Rogers, Toussaint had planned, after Haiti was freed, to go to Dahomey, West Africa and use it as a base to fight the slave trade. He saved 6 Million dollars which he entrusted to Stephen Girard, a white American ship captain. After Toussaint's capture, Girard refused to deliver the money to Toussaint's family. Girard became the richest American of his day. He left millions on his death in 1831 for the founding of Girard College in Philadelphia stipulating that it should be for whites only. He also gave money to buy coal for the poor whites of Philadelphia.

HARRIET TUBMAN - LEADER OF HUNDREDS OF SLAVES TO FREEDOM ON THE UNDERGROUND RAILROAD

The anniversary of the death of Harriet Tubman is March 10, 1913 who was the leader of hundreds of slaves to freedom. Harriet Tubman was born into slavery in Dorchester County, Maryland, and is known for having been the greatest conductor of the Underground Railroad.

In 1848, she successfully escaped despite the threat from her husband to report her to the slavemaster. A compassionate and extraordinarily brave woman, Tubman returned to the South some 20 times over the next ten years and helped more than 300 slaves escape to their freedom. She caused such a stir that a bounty of $40,000 was placed on her head.

As a participant during the civil war, Tubman served the Union Army as a nurse, soldier, spy and scout because of her successful routes with the Underground Railroad. Among her many honors, she was awarded a medal from Queen Victoria of England. Some 30 years after the civil war, Tubman received a pension of $20 a month for the rest of her life and used the money to fund a place for the aged and needy. The house was later named in her honor, "The Harriet Tubman Home," in Boston, Massachusetts.

MARY JOHNSON AND HER SON, WILLIAM
FREEDOM IS A BIRTHRIGHT

In 1820, Mary Johnson's former owner, a wealthy planter, decided to free her son William. However, the complex laws of the day required Blacks to post bonds guaranteeing their character as free persons of color. Neither slave parents nor their children could post bonds because the law required adults of color to be bonded or sponsor themselves, and as parents they had insufficient legal standing to take custody of their own children.

But the planter, William Johnson got the Legislature to pass a special law all his own. On January 21, 1820, William Johnson presented an eloquent petition to the Mississippi Assembly's Lower House for the boy's freedom and declared that he was acting to give "Liberty to a human being which all are entitled to as a birthright." A special Bill was passed and approved by the Governor on February 10, 1820, giving young William his freedom.

Using the former master's surname, young William Johnson became well known in business and letters as William Johnson, the "Diarist of Natchez", a literary success.

CLARA BROWN
"NOT WITHOUT MY DAUGHTER"

Clara Brown was born into slavery in Gallatin, Tennessee in 1800. Married and the mother of four children, one of whom died at birth in 1835, Brown suffered the pain of many Black mothers during slavery the pain of being separated from her children through a Kentucky slave auction.

Determined to one day be reunited with her children, and following the death of her master in 1857, Clara headed West in search of her daughter, Eliza. Walking most of the 600 mile trip as the only Black member of a wagon train, she settled in Central City, Colorado. In anticipation of purchasing her family's freedom, Clara opened a laundry to earn money.

As a member of the community, she won high praise for befriending her neighbors in a multitude of ways, including feeding the hungry and serving as a midwife. After the Civil War, Clara returned to Kentucky in search of her daughter. Unsuccessful, she returned to Central City with 16 freed slaves, some of which were orphans.

Finally in 1882, a friend of Clara's located Eliza living in Council Bluffs, Iowa, and at long last mother and daughter were reunited. Clara Brown survived probably by using the phrase long before the movie "Not without my Daughter."

UNCLE TOM - DESTROYING THE MYTH

Thousands of books, motion pictures, plays and individual comments have twisted the image of a positive Black Leader - Reverend Josiah Henson, known as "UNCLE TOM".

The real story of Uncle Tom was based on the life of Rev. Josiah Henson, a Black man who was born into slavery on June 15, 1789. After witnessing a tragedy involving his father, who was then separated from the family, Josiah grew to adulthood where he married and at the same time he was admitted as a minister in the Methodist Episcopal Church.

Josiah's slave master entrusted him to take and sell other slaves in another state and return with the money from the slave market to his original plantation. As he traveled, he began to think about purchasing his own freedom. He preached in various churches as he moved across the country and saved his collections to purchase his freedom.

When he returned to the Riley Plantation, the slave owner tricked him and took his money. Rev. Henson never received his freedom papers. After being in slavery for 41 years and deceived by his master, Rev. Henson took his wife and family and with the help of friendly Indians, walked from Kentucky to Canada. Believing that Canada was a safe place for African people, he returned to Kentucky as an agent of the Underground Railroad and freed 30 Kentucky slaves in 14 days and helped another 118 slaves escape to freedom.

His roots now firmly planted in Canadian soil as Rev. Josiah Henson - not Uncle Tom - Rev. Henson continued the struggle for the rights of African people until he died, preaching that Black people must become financially independent from white people before they can be truly free.

Remember a positive image of a positive Black Leader - when using the term "UNCLE TOM" - REV. JOSIAH HENSON.

NKYINKYIMIE

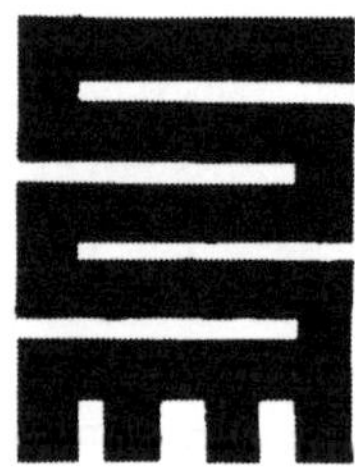

"Chance has never yet satisfied
the hope of a suffering people.
Action, self-reliance, the vision of self and
the future have been the only means
by which the oppressed have seen and
realized the light of their own freedom."

—*Marcus Mosias Garvey*

DAMEDAME

SYMBOLIZES: *CRAFTINESS AND INTELLIGENCE*

CHAPTER FOUR

1. ANNA MURRAY DOUGLASS
2. JOHN JAMES AUDUBON
3. BENJAMIN BANNEKER
4. THOMAS FULLER
5. PHILIP REED
6. ELLEN CRAFT
7. MARY FIELDS
8. ELLEN FREEMAN

ANNA MURRAY DOUGLASS - THE BETTER HALF OF FREDERICK DOUGLASS AND BACKBONE OF THE FAMILY

Because of her husband, Frederick Augustus Washington Bailey's prominent place in American Black History, it is easy to see how Anna Murray could easily be over shadowed. However, because of her tremendous courage, loyalty, love, and support for Bailey, she, too, has secured a place in history.

It was through Murray's financial efforts that Bailey was able to escape from Baltimore to New York disguised as a sailor. Upon his safe arrival, she joined him and they were married. They assumed the name "Johnson", but after meeting Nathan Johnson of New Bedford, Massachusetts, he formally introduced the new couple as Mr. and Mrs. Frederick Douglass.

While Frederick traveled, Anna provided comfort and shelter to hundreds of runaway slaves at their Rochester, New York home, which served as a station on the Underground Railroad. Although illiterate, she was the family's financial manager and maintained rock solid stability, during Frederick's absence.

Stricken with paralysis, Anna Murray Douglass, a devoted wife and mother of four, died in their Washington, D.C. home in 1882. Anna Murray Douglass - the "better half" of Frederick Douglass and the financial backbone of the family.

JOHN JAMES AUDUBON
THE BIRD MAN OF THE AUDUBON SOCIETY

John James Audubon was born on April 25, 1785, in Haiti. He was the son of a French Merchant Sea Captain and his African-Caribbean mistress. Taken to France following the death of his mother, Audubon was formally adopted by the Captain's legal wife. As a young boy, he developed a love of birds and began to collect them as subjects for his paintings.

After being sent to America in 1803, to escape enrollment in Napoleon's army, Audubon later married and moved to Kentucky. There he opened a general store, gave art lessons, worked as a taxidermist and painted. Traveling down the Mississippi, he once again began to collect bird specimens in order to draw them. For his drawings, he insisted on plates which were a specific size to capture the birds lifelike size.

Audubon later left America for England where he found his work to be more appreciated. Audubon died on January 27, 1851. Thirty-Five years after his death, a man named George Grinell founded an organization for the protection of birds. He named it "The Audubon Society, in honor of John James Audubon.

BENJAMIN BANNEKER
SCIENTIST, MATHEMATICIAN, ASTRONOMER, ARCHITECT AND INVENTOR

Benjamin Banneker was born near Baltimore, Maryland in 1731. He was taught to read and write by his grandmother, an English woman. It was discovered that he was a very gifted student, and at an early age he attended a small Quaker School for Blacks and whites where he developed a keen insight into science and mathematics, teaching himself astronomy. A genius at mathematics and astronomy, he predicted the solar eclipse of 1789.

He became the first Black Presidential Appointee in the United States when he was appointed as a surveyor on the six-man team formed to design the blue prints for the U.S. Capitol, the Treasury Building, and the White House and is responsible for completing the architectural layout of Washington, D.C. Banneker invented and built the first wooden clock in the United States, from the design of a pocket watch given to him. This wooden clock kept perfect time for forty years.

From 1791 to 1796, Banneker made tide calculations and weather predictions for a yearly almanac. When the almanac was published in 1792, Banneker sent a copy of it with a letter to President Thomas Jefferson, who was a slaveholder, challenging him to use his influence to put an end to slavery which he never did.

THOMAS FULLER
THE AFRICAN CALCULATOR

Heavyweight champion, Muhammad Ali in his boxing career would predict the round when he would either knock his opponent out or when the fight would end. This method of calculating was following in the tradition of Thomas Fuller - The African Calculator.

Thomas Fuller - the African Calculator could figure sums involving billions in his head faster than others could with a pencil. Born into slavery, he could give the diameter of the earth in inches despite interruptions. When he was asked the question of how many seconds in a year and a half, he replied in two minutes, 47,304,000, counting 365 days to the year.

When Fuller was asked how many seconds a man would have lived, aged seventy-four years, seventeen days and 12 hours, he replied in a minute and a half, the answer: 2,210,500,800 seconds. In a contest with a white opponent, who had a pen and paper, Fuller was asked the question of how many seconds in seventy years, and he won. The opponent lost by inadvertently omitting the leap years.

When Thomas Fuller passed away, it was acknowledged that Fuller having lived in slavery and oppression and been denied the opportunities of a free individual, but was considered by the scholars of the time, as a "Brother in Science" Thomas Fuller, the African Calculator.

PHILIP REED AND THE CAPITOL BUILDING

Washington, D.C. - The Nation's Capitol. Did you know that the most famous structures in DC - the White House and the Capitol Building were built by slave labor? It was a slave, who as a highly skilled mechanic, performed the difficult task of fitting the statue of freedom on the dome of the Capitol.

Philip Reed as a slave was owned and worked for a foundry owned by a Mr. Mills. During the time of construction of the Capitol Building, the foreman and superintendent of the construction working on the dome of the Capitol, decided to strike for ten dollars instead of the eight dollars they were paid. Philip Reed took his place as superintendent and continued the work. Reed raised the statue, bolted the joints together and had the huge mass of construction lifted into place.

The Capitol library lists the name of Philip Reed as being responsible for this construction. Reed attained his freedom and went into business for himself. Philip Reed - expert and master construction worker in the history of the Nation's Capitol.

ELLEN CRAFT
THE CRAFTY ESCAPE TO FREEDOM

Ellen Craft was born into slavery to her African mother and white slaveowner in Clinton, Georgia; and, was often mistaken as an immediate member of the master's family. She met her husband, William Craft after being given away to a family in Macon, Georgia. Together, the couple pulled off one of the most daring escapes from slavery ever recorded.

Ellen posed as a young, white sickly male slaveowner traveling with "his" slave. The mere thought of bearing children into slavery and having them possibly separated from her was Ellen Craft's strength and determination. Ellen's role was made increasingly difficult because she had to pose first, as a white man, and second as an educated one.

Their plan was to travel by train and steamer through Georgia to reach Philadelphia. Close calls and quick thinking by Ellen helped them throughout the eight day ordeal. One event saw her play deaf and answer with only one word to avoid recognition by a man who knew her and her slaveowners. High profile because of their extraordinary escape, and the passage of the Fugitive Slave Law of 1850 (The law allowing slavecatchers to return runaway slaves to their owners) the couple left Boston upon hearing their former owners had hired slavecatchers to return them.

Successful in a second escape, they went to England. Eighteen years later, with two children, the Crafts returned to America and told their remarkable story in detail in a book called "RUNNING A THOUSAND MILES FOR FREEDOM."

MARY FIELDS
MAIL CARRIER AND SUPER PIONEER WOMAN

Mary Fields escaped to freedom from Tennessee to Ohio in 1855. Standing six foot, 200 pounds, cigar smoking, whisky drinking, two fisted, gun-toting, Mary Fields was a Pioneer Woman who settled her arguments with her fists and at times, with her six gun.

Alluding slavecatchers in 1884, Mary moved to Cascade, Montana, where she worked for St. Peter's Mission School. Her job involved loading and unloading freight to various communities in Montana. Until help arrived, Mary Fields fought off wolf packs, which would frighten the horses and cause them to bolt. She was caught in several snow storms that reduced visibility to zero. Forced to stop in sub-zero weather, she moved briskly all night to keep from freezing to death. After a shootout and brawl with one of the hired hands at the mission, Mary left in 1895.

Mary Fields took a job with the United States Mail and made her deliveries on time in spite of weather for eight years. She retired at the age of 62. Still going strong, she owned a restaurant and slowing down at the age of 70, earned a living doing odd jobs. Demonstrating that she was still rough and tough, one afternoon when a man who had not paid her for his laundry passed the saloon, she saw him, overtook him and knocked him out, and returned to the bar to resume her socializing with her saloon friends saying "His laundry bill is paid". Super pioneer woman, Mary Fields, leaving her mark on the West, became known as "Black Mary"

ELIZABETH FREEMAN
ABOLITIONIST

Elizabeth Freeman was born into slavery in the home of Colonel John Ashley during the time when American colonies were becoming more and more dissatisfied with British rule. The Ashley household constantly talked about liberty, freedom and equality but not particularly for slaves.

In an attempt to gain her freedom, Ms. Freeman left the Ashley household after the Revolutionary War ended. Arguing the principles of the Declaration of Independence, "Mum Bett" as she was known, convinced a young lawyer named Theodore Sedgwick to take her case before the Courts.

In her case BROM AND BETT v. J. ASHLEY, ESQ. heard by the County Court of Great Barrington, Massachusetts, is where she raised the point that as a result of the American Revolution, slavery was illegal and she should be free. As a direct result of her case, Elizabeth was granted freedom and slavery in Massachusetts ended. She adopted the last name Freeman upon winning her case.

Elizabeth Freeman died December 28, 1829. Fighting for her freedom through the legal system, this extraordinary lady was the great-grandmother of another great African American hero, W.E.B. DuBois.

DAMEDAME

*"One's work may be finished some day,
but one's education never."*

—ALEXANDER DUMAS

*"Education is our passport to the future,
for tomorrow belongs to the people
who prepare for it today."*

—EL-HAJJ MALIK EL-SHABAZZ
(MALCOLM X)

DWENNIMMEN

SYMBOLIZES: ***HUMILITY AND STRENGTH, WISDOM AND LEARNING***

CHAPTER FIVE

1. HENRY E. BAKER
2. PAUL CUFFE
3. JAMES FORTEN
4. SUSIE KING TAYLOR
5. ALEXANDER PUSKIN
6. PRINCE HALL
7. DR. DANIEL HALE WILLIAMS
8. GEORGIA L. PATTON WASHINGTON

HENRY E. BAKER
THE PRINCIPLE OF PURPOSE

Henry Baker is responsible for the accurate recording of the inventions and contributions of African Americans at a time when no one else thought it necessary. Born in the pre-Civil War Mississippi, he attended school in Columbus before being admitted in 1875 to the United States Naval Academy.

In 1877, he took a position as a "Copyist" at the Patent Office in Washington, D.C. and began attending the Ben-Hyde Benton School of Technology. Two years later, he entered Harvard University Law School, and in 1881, rose to the position of Second Assistant Examiner in the Patent Office.

While employed, he made his purpose in life to compile four large volumes of actual patent drawings of inventions that he knew were patented by Black men and women. Racism was a factor in preventing Baker from recording many of the inventions held by Black patentees because when Baker wrote to inventors, he was informed that acknowledging that they were Black would affect the commercial value of their invention.

Because of this Baker could not list all of the inventions patented in the 1800s, but he never concluded his research in this field. Henry E. Baker - keeping the record of African American inventors.

PAUL CUFFE
MERCHANT, ABOLITIONIST

Paul Cuffe was born a free child in 1759 on Chuttyhunk Island, Massachusetts. His father Kofi was a member of the Ashanti of West Africa, who was captured and brought to America as a slave at the age of ten.

A skilled carpenter, Kofi (Cuffe) earned his freedom and educated himself. Following his father's death, Paul signed up on a whaling vessel and later cargo ships, where he learned navigational skills. With the outbreak of the American Revolution, he and his brother built a boat and began their trading business, which included running British blockades with American supplies. This small business gradually became a large fleet of merchant vessels including his own shipyard, which helped make him one of the wealthiest men in America.

Although wealthy, he was concerned about the unfair treatment of Blacks both free and slave and in 1780 petitioned the Council of Bristol County to end Taxation without representation for Blacks denied the right to vote. But his largest crusade took shape in the form of a "Back to Africa" campaign. On December 10, 1815 after four years of exploratory research and much of his wealth invested, he set sail for Sierra Leone, Africa with a group of free Blacks. His intent was to end slavery at the West African Colony by building a free and prosperous industrialized Africa. Despite difficulties by white merchants, the African American group prospered. Returning to America, Paul Cuffe died on September 1, 1817.

JAMES FORTEN
A SAILOR AND HUMAN RIGHTS ACTIVIST

James Forten is an African American inventor who is credited with the invention of an apparatus for managing sails of ships.

James Forten was born free in Philadelphia and lived from 1766 to 1842. He served with the Navy during the War of Independence. During his service in the Navy he developed a device for handling the sails of ships. He became the leading sailmaking shop in Philadelphia and financially wealthy and independent.

As an African American born free during the time of slavery his personal success did not blind him to the evils of slavery, and he used his money to secure the rights of other African Americans still in slavery and to fight for women's rights, temperance and peace. He was one of the organizers of the convention of free "Negroes" in 1830. James Forten - A successful business man, but a human rights activist for the rights of African American people.

SUSIE KING TAYLOR
NURSE, ACTIVIST, AUTHOR AND TEACHER

Susie Baker was born into slavery in 1848 in Savannah, Georgia and learned how to read and write through her own efforts and with the help of several other individuals. Encouraged by her grandmother, Susie used her skills to help her friends by producing written passes for slaves and freemen.

Once the Civil War began, Susie and an uncle escaped to St. Catherine's Island where they were under the protection of the Union Fleet and part of a experiment in freedom where sympathetic Northern commanders gave freed Black people land and encouraged them to become self-sufficient.

Susie married, started a school for children and adults and became associated with the first Black Regiment formed in the South. Serving first as a laundress, she learned how to use a rifle, cooked for the wounded and taught Black Soldiers how to read and write. As the casualties increased, Susie King became the camp nurse. She returned to Savannah where Mrs. King opened a night school for adults.

After the tragedy of losing her husband in an accident, she moved to Boston remarried and wrote her autobiography to awaken the social consciousness within America.

ALEXANDER PUSHKIN FATHER OF RUSSIAN LITERATURE

Alexander Pushkin is to Russia what Shakespeare is to English literature and he is considered the "Father of Russian Literature". Of African heritage, Pushkin was born in Moscow on May 26, 1799. The second of three children, went to a school for bright children and was trained to be a civil servant.

Although he was related to many rich and influential people in Russia, Pushkin's heart was with the poorest people in the countryside. He expressed his feelings at the age of 15 when he wrote his first poem which was written in Russian. This was a big event because everyone else had always written in French. With this poem he set free the Russian spoken word. He became a champion of the rich and poor people and gave them a new pride in Russia and its culture. They were no longer ashamed of their own language, thanks to his poems. Pushkin proved to the Russian people that the Russian language was worth having and at the age of 18 was the most talked about poet in Russia. He wrote about the struggles of the poor, which was very brave because those who spoke out against the government were sent to Siberia, a cold and lonely place, a punishment worse than death.

While belonging to a secret society formed to do away with the government, over 100 of his friends were sent to Siberia. Pushkin escaped by being out of the city at the time of an uprising. A year later, when questioned by the Czar ("ZAR") of his participation, he admitted to being a part of the secret society, however, the Czar was grateful for what Pushkin had done for Russia and named him the Imperial Historian. At the age of 31, he married one of Russia's most beautiful women, and died on January 19, 1937 defending her honor at the age of 37. His poetry is considered a symbol of genius and in Russian he is known as " The Father of Russian Literature". Despite being born in Russia, he was known to be proud of his African heritage blood.

PRINCE HALL
FOUNDER OF THE BLACK MASONS

Prince Hall was born in Barbados and moved to Cambridge, Massachusetts in 1765. Within ten years, he became a Methodist Minister and leader in the Black Community. As a free Black person, he made it a point to sign petitions against slavery and made public protests against racial discrimination. Prince Hall also served in the Revolution and saw action at Bunker Hill.

But Prince Hall was also a pioneer organizer. As the father of Black secret fraternal societies in America, Prince Hall began a new development during the Revolutionary War period of Black organizations, led by Blacks and designed to promote racial unity and self-improvement. Prince Hall succeeded in obtaining a charter from England enabling him to set up African Lodge No. 489 in Boston in 1787.

Four years later, he became the first Grand Master of the Black Masons, an office he held until his death in 1807. Prince Hall - Founder of the Black Masons in the United States.

DR. DANIEL HALE WILLIAMS
MASTER OF HEART SURGERY

Dr. Daniel Hale Williams performed the first open heart surgery in 1893 in the United States. Dr. Williams was born in Pittsburgh, Pennsylvania on January 18, 1858. Losing his parents at the age of 12, he earned his way through a local academy in Wisconsin by working as a barber. With the help of friends he graduated from Chicago Medical School in 1883. Eight years later, Dr. Williams founded Provident Hospital.

On March 27, 1893, Williams saved the life of a knifing victim by "sewing up his heart". Working in a makeshift operating room too small for the six-man operating team, he skillfully exposed the pulsating heart and stitched the wound a fraction of an inch from the heart, all without the aid of X-rays, blood transfusions or modern "miracle drugs". Dr. Williams risked his job and the life of his hospital to save the patient.

Fifty-one days later, the patient, James Cornish, was released from Dr. Williams hospital. Two years later, the doctor saw Cornish working in a stockyard, and fifty-one years later, Cornish was living a normal, happy life, outliving the man who saved his life - Dr. Daniel Hale Williams - the master of open heart surgery.

GEORGIA E.L. PATTON WASHINGTON
FROM SLAVE TO DOCTOR IN THE HOUSE

Georgia L. Patton Washington was born into slavery on April 16, 1864 in Grundy County, Tennessee. Four years after entering Central Tennessee College in Nashville in 1886, Georgia L. Patton completed her course work and entered the Meharry Medical Department of Central Tennessee College, currently known as Meharry Medical College. Upon graduation in 1893, Patton started a number of "FIRSTS" including being the first Black woman to graduate from Meharry Medical College.

Two months following her graduation, without any financial support from her church missionary society, she journeyed to Africa as a self-supporting missionary, making her the first Meharry graduate to serve as a missionary in Africa. Her cabinmate aboard the ship was a young antilynching lecturer and journalist, Ida B. Wells. Her work benefited over a hundred individuals in Monrovia, Liberia, but after two years her health started failing and she returned to America.

Opening a medical practice in Memphis, Georgia Patton became the first Black woman to be licensed and practice as a physician and surgeon in the State, and the first to practice in Memphis. She later married David W. Washington, who was the first Black hired as a letter carrier in the City. Unfortunately, the couple lost two children after their birth. On November 8, 1900 Georgia E. L. Patton Washington died at the age of 36.

DWENNIMMEN

"We must not only be able to wear black boots, but to make them."
—Frederick Douglass

"It is the fool whose own tomatoes are sold to him."
—Unknown

AYA

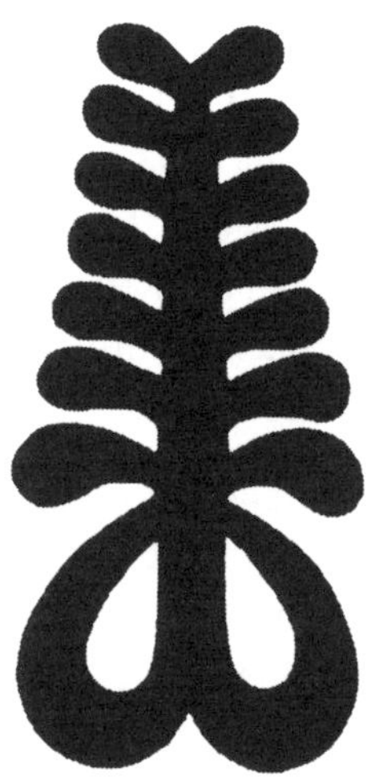

SYMBOLIZES: *ENDURANCE AND DEFIANCE*

CHAPTER SIX

1. IDA B. WELLS
2. JENNY SLEW
3. JAMES ROBINSON
4. ANNE HAMPTON AND SOLOMON NORTHRUP
5. JOHN READ
6. WILLIS AND ELSIE HAMILTON
7. MISS MARY HAMILTON
8. MR. REYMOND

IDA B. WELLS - THE LONELY WARRIOR / LET THE RECORD BE KNOWN

Ida B. Wells was born in 1864 in Holly Springs, Mississippi. Losing both her parents at age 14 during the yellow fever epidemic of 1878, she raised four younger brothers and sisters. Attending Rust College and later Fisk, she taught in county schools in both Mississippi and Tennessee. During this time, she became very outspoken against the injustices towards Blacks, which ultimately caused her to lose her job.

At the age of twenty-two, she successfully sued the Chesapeake, Ohio and the Southwestern Railroad Companies for refusing to provide her the first class accommodations for which she had paid. Moving to Memphis, Wells became part-owner and editor of the newspaper FREE SPEECH, for which she further used as a device to spread her message of inequality. One such message was carried in her pamphlet, THE RED RECORD, in which Wells spoke out against lynching. As a crusader, she was concerned for the protection of Black People being lynched from 1877 and reported the gross injustices inflicted upon Black citizens. Not just confined to the South, Wells also spoke out in Northern cities as well as Europe.

Ida B. Wells co-founded the NAACP, and assisted in organizing the first Black Women's Club, and the Alpha Suffrage Club of Chicago, the first Black Women's Political Club. In 1990 the U.S. Postal Service paid tribute to her by commissioning a stamp to the greatest anti-lynching crusader and heroine freedom fighter in African American history to let the record be known.

JENNY SLEW AND ANNIVERSARY OF THE 13TH AMENDMENT

January 24th is the anniversary of the 13th Amendment passed by Congress to abolish slavery in 1865. According to Webster's Dictionary, slavery is defined as the "Ownership of a person or persons by another or others" and "Severe toil; drudgery".

There were several individual slaves who made efforts to obtain their freedom through legal means and were successful. One of the more prominent cases or "Freedom Suits" involved a woman slave, named Jenny Slew, who in 1766, sued her master, John Whipple of Massachusetts, charging him with restraining her liberty. Jenny Slew not only won her freedom, but in addition, the court awarded her "The sum of Four Pounds" in damages.

Jenny Slew's victory led to a large number of individual freedom suits throughout the North. Although most were successful, the legal route toward freedom was time-consuming, and was expensive, with legal fees and related expenses more than the average slave could afford, with the duration of 500 years of slavery, the Revolutionary War and the Civil War. However, on January 24, 1865, Congress passed the 13th Amendment to abolish slavery in the United States. This amendment legalized and fortified the Emancipation Proclamation and prohibited slavery or involuntary servitude, except as a punishment for crime, in all parts of the United States.

JAMES ROBINSON - SOLDIER AMERICAN REVOLUTION AND WAR OF 1812

James Robinson, born into slavery in Mayland was a soldier in the American Revolution and War of 1812. In return for fighting during the American Revolution, many slaves were promised their freedom. One such slave who fought for America's freedom, as well as his own, was James Robinson. Upon winning a Gold Medal for Military Valor at the Battle of Yorktown, awarded to him by the French Commander Lafayette, he was returned to slavery. His return to slavery was due to the death of his original master and the heirs refused to honor the promise of freedom.

Despite his obvious disappointment, when Andrew Jackson called for volunteers in support of the War of 1812 to defend New Orleans, Robinson again answered the call. When the fighting was over, he was once again returned to slavery. After years of servitude, at the age of 110, James Robinson was finally able to live as a free man with the signing of the Emancipation Proclamation. He died at the age of 115 after moving to Detroit, Michigan.

ANNE HAMPTON AND SOLOMON NORTHRUP TRUE LOVE

Anne Hampton and Solomon Northrup pledged their eternal love and were wed on December 25, 1828 unaware that their love would be tested. Living as free persons of color in New York in January, 1841, Solomon was offered a job as a part-time violinist with a traveling band. He was tricked, kidnapped, beaten and sold into slavery in New Orleans. Solomon wrote his wife to inform her of what had happened but was unable to tell his location. He was sold and resold.

Anne failed in tracing Solomon for eleven years but in September 1852 he sent a second letter with a Louisiana postmark. On November 19, 1852 Anne Northrup petitioned the Governor of New York to aid in her husband's rescue.

In January, 1853, twelve years after his kidnapping Solomon came home to Anne a free man. Solomon published his story, titled TWELVE YEARS A SLAVE. That publication aided in capturing his kidnappers. The Northrups, Anne and Solomon had true love.

JOHN READ
I AIN'T GOING OUT LIKE THAT

John Read as a free man was to uneasy and unable to sleep on the night of December 14, 1820 at his home in Kennet Township, Pennsylvania. He got up, made a fire and by midnight heard people outside. Fearing slave catchers were attempting to return him to the life of slavery and always protecting himself, he was armed and asked if there was a search warrant after being informed that they were looking for stolen goods.

The attackers stormed the door and he warned that he would shoot if they came in because "It is life for life". They did not believe he would shoot and as the first entered, Read shot and as the next one rushed in he clubbed him and took his gun. Escaping to a home of a neighbor he explained that he had been attacked and killed two and he did not want to be hunted so he waited to be arrested.

When officials searched his home, they found the two bodies, pistols, handcuffs, a whip and a rope. Read was charged with manslaughter in the kidnapper-agent's death and sentenced to nine years in prison. Even in 1820, living in a free state there was no justice for Black people, but at least Read lived to tell the story.

WILLIS AND ELSIE HAMILTON
I AINT GOING

Willis and Elise Hamilton were fugitive/runaway slaves who were saved from slave catchers by Laura Haviland, a white resident of Adrian, Michigan who was a staunch abolitionist. Slaveowners offered a reward of $3,000 Dead or Alive, and even though Laura Haviland had threats on her life, she harbored fugitive slaves and helped them reach free soil by way of the Underground Railroad.

Laura Haviland was kidnapped and held captive by slave catchers who ordered her to write a letter and tell the fugitive family to come to Toledo, Ohio where "Aunt Laura" Haviland was being held. She wrote Willis and Elsie Hamilton offering clothes for her daughters and described "a black dress in the South bedroom, two pink aprons and a striped green dress in the West bedroom," etc.

When the letter was delivered and read, Elsie said to her husband, "I shall not stir a step. This is a humbug. Mrs. Haviland does not have a black dress, no south bedroom, no pink aprons or any green striped dresses." Willis and Elsie Hamilton were never captured, but today, in Adrian, Michigan, there is a statue of "Aunt Laura" Haviland in one of the public squares.

MISS MARY HAMILTON - AND SELF RESPECT

Miss Mary Hamilton was on the witness stand in a local Alabama Court on September 26, 1963 when a prosecutor insisted on referring to Miss Hamilton by her first name. She agreed to answer all questions only if properly addressed as Miss Hamilton. The questioning never got beyond her name, the judge intervened and cited Miss Hamilton for contempt of court, sentencing her to five days in jail and a $50 fine.

The court transcript is clear that the prosecutor continued to provoke the witness. Miss Hamilton made her point equally clear and appealed her conviction to the Alabama State Appellate Court, Alabama State Supreme Court and up to the United States Supreme Court where the judgment was handed down on March 30, 1964.

The judgment was reversed giving victory to a Black Woman who had a right to her name - Miss Mary Hamilton who was willing to go to the extent of the law and demand respect for herself, and set a legal precedent for us all.

MR. REYMOND
YOU CAN'T MAKE ME A SLAVE FOR LIFE

In 1832 Mr. Reymond, a self-emancipated man from slavery, was a member of a group, The New York Vigilance Committee which was committed to sabotaging slavery and protected over 335 persons from slavery. By 1837 in New York, slavery had been abolished over ten years, but the State of New York still did not meet minimum standards of justice for freeman and ex-slaves.

At a New York meeting of Blacks, Reymond offered news of a colony of escaped slaves and freeborn Blacks. Slave Catchers' spies reported his name and remarks in a newspaper. A copy was sent to his hometown, Norfolk, Virginia, and the Mayor issued a warrant for Reymond's immediate arrest. When Reymond was returned to Norfolk, he was asked a trick question, `If he had been out of the state for over a year'. This was to establish that he was an escaped slave. He answered "Yes" and was imprisoned with no chance to defend himself. No one claimed him and 24 hours later he was released and forever banished from Virginia. All this happened because he had spoken out at a meeting in a free state.

In 1837, free Blacks found liberty meaningless with the growth of the slave trade. To speak in public, sign a petition, sign a church notice, enroll a child in school or advertise a business, free Blacks risked being captured and taken back into slavery. But Mr. Reymond beat the odds.

AYA

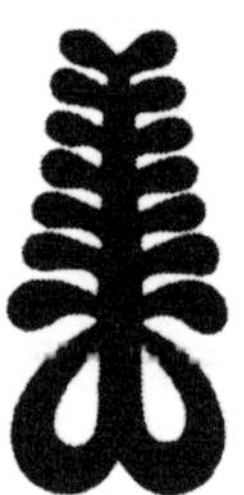

"If there is no struggle, There is no progress.
Those who profess to favor freedom,
and yet deprecate agitation, are men who want
crops without thunder and lightning.
They want the ocean without the awful roar
of its many waters. This struggle may be a moral one;
or it may be a physical one; or it may be both
moral and physical; but it must be a struggle.
Power concedes nothing without a demand."

—FREDERICK DOUGLASS

HWEMUDUA

SYMBOLIZES: ***THE BELIEF IN THE BEST THAT CAN BE OF EVERYTHING AND THERE IS NO TOLERANCE OF IMPERFECTION.***

CHAPTER SEVEN

1. U.S. CONGRESSMAN GEORGE WASHINGTON MURRAY
2. JAN MATZELIGER
3. NORBET RILLIEUX
4. GEORGE WASHINGTON CARVER
5. JACK JOHNSON
6. ELIJAH McCOY
7. DR. SHIRLEY A. JACKSON
8. DR. BENJAMIN S. CARSON

U.S. CONGRESSMAN GEORGE WASHINGTON MURRAY AN INVENTOR IN THE 1890s

During the late 1880s African Americans were organizing independent Black Expositions and Fairs. During this reconstruction period, legislation was being proposed sponsoring the Cotton States Exhibition which would publicize the South's Technological progress since the Civil War.

So, on August 10, 1894, on the floor of the House of Representatives, George Washington Murray, an African American Congressman from South Carolina, placed the names of 91 Black inventors in the Congressional Record. It was a testament to the technological achievement of a people who were recently emancipated from slavery.

Congressman George Washington Murray was himself responsible for 12 patents which include: Combined Furrow Opener, Stalk Knocker, Cultivator and Marker, Planter, Cotton Chopper, Fertilizing Distributor, among others.

George Washington Murray, U.S. Congressman, Inventor and advocate for the recording of African American technological achievement which is forever on the Congressional record.

JAN MATZELIGER THE SHOE MAN

Born on September 9, 1852 in Paramaribo, Surinam, South America, Jan Matzeliger immigrated to the United States. As a young man working in a shoe factory in Lynn, Massachusetts, he imagined a machine that could automatically produce shoes. With almost no support from his co-workers he began to make his vision a reality.

After approximately ten years of hard work, Matzeliger designed and built a machine that could adjust a shoe, arrange leather over the shoe, drive in the nails and deliver a finished product in less than a minute. This invention by Matzeliger fueled the industrial revolution by increasing shoe manufacturing production by more than 100%. Many people benefited from the invention through the reduction in shoe prices, increased wages and improved working conditions.

Jan Matzeliger died of tuberculosis on August 24, 1889 at the age of 37. Some years before his death, Matzeliger became a member of a white church in Lynn called The North Congregational Society and bequeathed some of the stock of the company he had organized. Years after his death, the church heavily in debt, remembering Jan Matzeliger, sold the stock and was able to pay off its debt. With the cancelled mortgage as one incentive, the Church held a special service of thanks one Sunday morning with a life size portrait of Jan Matzeliger.

Thanks to Jan Matzeliger the shoe lasting machine patented on March 20, 1883 revolutionized the shoe industry and made Lynn, Massachusetts the "Shoe Capital of the World".

NORBET RILLIEUX - INVENTOR OF THE EVAPORATION PAN HOW SWEET IT IS

In 1806, in New Orleans, one of America's first modern scientific geniuses was born - Norbet Rillieux. After studying engineering in France, he returned to Louisiana with his inventions that revolutionized the sugar industry of the world. He was the most sought-after engineer in the sugar-producing states, where the Department of Agriculture called his invention known as the "Multiple effect evaporation" - "The greatest invention in the history of chemical engineering."

African American workers were very thankful to Norbet for his invention because in order to make refined (white) sugar, the workers had to climb up long ladders attached to huge pots of boiling liquids. They used ladles to mix these liquids and had to transfer them from pot to pot. Many workers accidentally fell into the pots or were disfigured by the splashing liquids. With the simple turning of a few knobs, Norbet's invention reduced this dangerous process.

Unappreciated and unaccepted as a Black man in America, Norbet Rillieux moved to Europe where he was appreciated for his creative genius. His invention laid the foundation for all modern industrial evaporation and in the sugar industry saved the world trillions of dollars in lost lives and fuel.

GEORGE WASHINGTON CARVER

George Washington is best known for his invention of peanut butter, peanut oil but he also created over 300 inventions from the peanut, sweet potato and pecan.

Born into slavery near Diamond Grove, Missouri in 1864, Carver went on to finish high school and applied to a college in Iowa and was admitted. But when the President saw that Carver was an African American he did not admit him. To support his early years of education, Carver opened a laundry and later moved to Winterset, Iowa and also worked as first cook in a large hotel.

Carver later went on to attend Simpson College, Iowa, then Iowa State College, obtaining a Bachelor and Masters Degrees pursuing his agricultural work. At Tuskeegee Institute, he did productive agricultural research in nutrition, chemistry, genetics, plant pathology, soil fertilization and the use of waste products. Carver not only revealed medical properties in weeds, but created over 300 products from the peanut, 100 from the pecan and 118 products from the sweet potato.

George Washington Carver received only three patents for his work with the peanut for Cosmetics, Paint and Stains Process and the Process of Producing Paint. The other inventions were various such as:

Adhesives	Insulating Board	Shoe Polish
Axle Grease	Linoleum	Shaving Cream
Bleach	Mayonnaise	Sugar
Synthetic Rubber	Synthetic Marble	Metal Polish
Wood Filler	Paper	Dyes
Wood Stains	Imitation Oysters	Ink

Breakfast Food No. 5 with extra protein for diabetic people from skins of Peanut - Over 30 different dyes from black to orange/yellow.

This is a tribute to George Washington Carver, one of the greatest chemists of all time whose products and processes not only revolutionized the economy of the South but created countless new industries and laid the foundation or new fields in science.

JACK JOHNSON
THE INVENTOR/BOXER

Jack Johnson - was the boxer and the subject of the film - the Great White Hope which starred James Earl Jones. This film told Jack Johnson's life as a boxer ... But did not tell you that Jack Johnson received a patent on an improved type of monkeywrench in 1922.

Jack Johnson became the first Black Heavyweight Champion of the World and the first Black athlete known to openly defy the rules of behavior laid down by white America for Blacks. Not content with just having the title, the Texas-born champion made a habit of flaunting his success. When white Americans moved to crush him, they did so with all the brutality they could muster. Jack Johnson was arrested on trumped up charges of white slavery known as the Mann Act.

After jumping bail, driven into self-exile abroad, roaming from continent to continent, the ex-champ returned to his homeland where, after serving a year at Leavenworth, received a patent for the Improvement in the Monkeywrench. More than just a boxing champion, Jack Johnson can also be remembered for his innovative skill as an inventor.

ELIJAH McCOY
THE REAL McCOY

Elijah McCoy was born in Colcester, Ontario, Canada on May 2, 1844. He moved to Michigan after the Civil War. McCoy was employed as a rail-road engineer and one of McCoy's responsibilities was to keep the moving parts of the railroad engine lubricated. This tedious task inspired McCoy to automate the lubrication process, virtually ending the need to periodically stop an engine. McCoy's device was called the "Drip Cup". It was a tiny container filled with oil whose flow was regulated by means of a "Stopcock".

During McCoy's career, he received more than 56 patents for devices which were improved versions of his automatic lubrication process. His other inventions include the lawn sprinkler, ironing table and the Steam Cylinder Lubricator.

The high quality of Elijah McCoy's inventions gained such notoriety that the phrase "The Real McCoy" was coined to separate "The Father of Lubrication" inventions from cheap imitations.

DR. SHIRLEY A. JACKSON
SCIENTIST EXTRAORDINAIRE
THE TRUE VOICE

Dr. Shirley A. Jackson, a leading scientist in America is one of the greatest contributors to the "true voice" abilities of the telephone system. During her childhood she had an interest in science and math and conducted many different experiments. On the honors program throughout school, she enrolled in the Massachusetts Institute of Technology ("MIT"). She became the first African American woman to receive a Doctorate degree in the field of particle physics, an area of science that deals with matter and motion. Dr. Jackson also founded the first Black Student Union at MIT.

After college, Dr. Jackson also became a leading scientist by conducting successful experiments in theoretical physics. While working at Bell Laboratories, the research division of AT&T, Dr. Jackson worked on experiments involving condensed matter and semiconductors, and helped AT&T make many advances in the field of telecommunications. Included in this field are the development of the touch tone phone, portable fax, solar cell and fiber optic cables used to provide clear sound in overseas telephone calls. Dr. Jackson received numerous awards, including the 1973 "Scientist of the Year Award". Without the help of Dr. Shirly A. Jackson, we would not have call waiting, caller ID, as well as talking on the phone without a noisy background.

DR. BENJAMIN S. CARSON
GIFTED HANDS

When eight years old, Dr. Benjamin S. Carson, lived in a poor Detroit neighborhood, and was raised in a single parent home, where his mother took domestic jobs to support her two sons. She made her sons read at least two books a week and write her a report on each to instill the importance of education. Carson as a poor student graduated third in his high school class and won a scholarship to Yale University. After graduating, he entered the University of Michigan School of Medicine.

In 1984, he was appointed director of Pediatric Neurosurgery at John Hopkins University Hospital in Baltimore at the age of 33 years old, the youngest person in the country to hold that position. Dr. Carson made medical history in 1985 by performing a medical procedure of removing half the brain of a four year old girl who was suffering from 150 seizures a day. The other half of her brain took over all functions and the girl went on to grow and develop normally.

Carson again made medical history in 1987 when he led the medical team who successfully separated Siamese twins joined at the head.

Carson wrote his autobiography, GIFTED HANDS, and his motivational book THINK BIG outlining his philosophy for a successful life.

HWEMUDUA

"Every race and every nation should be judged by the best it has been able to produce, not by the worst."
—JAMES WELDON JOHNSON

NTESIE

SYMBOLIZES: ***WISDOM, KNOWLEDGE AND PRUDENCE***

CHAPTER EIGHT

1. GRANVILLE T. WOODS
2. THOMAS L. JENNINGS
3. ANNIE TURNBO MALONE
4. FREDERICK McKINLEY JONES
5. HERMON L. GRIMES
6. ANN MOORE
7. LONNIE JOHNSON
8. MORRIS B. WILLIAMS

GRANVILLE T. WOODS
INVENTOR

Granville T. Woods was born on April 23, 1856 in Columbus, Ohio. Entering College, Woods studied Mechanical Engineering and ultimately developed over 80 inventions during his 20 year career. One of his most noted inventions was the Synchronos Multiplex Railway Telegraph, a device which enabled moving trains to communicate with one another, helping to avoid possible accidents.

Another invention was his electric generator, which was patented on November 4, 1896. The device was used to vary, as desired, the strength of the electrical current delivered to a required device thus preventing the over-heating and burnouts of resistors. The significance of this invention was that it reduced the number of fires due to resistors overheating and led to a 40% savings in electricity.

Other inventions included a steam boiler furnace, an incubator, and an automatic air brake system. During the height of his career the American Catholic Tribune called Woods "The Greatest Electrician in the World."

THOMAS JENNINGS
FATHER OF THE CLEANERS AND ABOLITIONIST

In 1821, Thomas Jennings is known as the first African American to receive a patent for his invention. He was issued a patent for a dry-cleaning process known as "Dry Scouring". Jennings owned a dry cleaning and tailoring business in New York City and was said to have used most of his profits to support the abolitionist cause.

An activist for the rights of his people, Jennings served as Assistant Secretary of the First Annual Convention of the People of Color in June 1831 in Philadelphia.

His daughter, following in his footsteps broke up the Jim-Crow car in New York. When she was removed from the "white only" car one Sunday morning, she employed Chester Arthur, later President of the United States to take her case to the Supreme Court and won.

Thomas Jennings, the inventor of the dry cleaning process, and an unsung hero and champion for the human rights of African people in 1821.

ANNIE TURNBO MALONE ENTREPRENEUR AND PHILANTHROPIST

Annie Turnbo Malone was born on August 9, 1869 in Metropolis, Illinois. There are historical sources that credit Malone as being this country's first Black Millionairess even though many sources cite Madame C.J. Walker, who prior to starting her business in hair care was a student of Annie Malone. During the 1920s, Malone was reported to be worth 14 million dollars which was made from the development of non-damaging hair straighten products, hair growers and conditioners.

Under the name "Poro" she built a financial empire and Poro College in 1917 aimed at educating the Black community in St. Louis. The College trained women as agents for Poro products and by 1926 claimed to have graduated 75,000 agents throughout the world including the Caribbean.

Her contributions in giving back to the community are recorded. She supported two full time students in every Black land-grant college in the nation during the 1920s and donated $25,000 to Howard University which at that time was the largest gift ever by a Black American to a Black College.

Annie Malone died on May 10, 1957 of a stroke in Chicago's Provident Hospital, founded by Dr. Daniel Hale Williams, the African American who performed the first open heart surgery.

FREDERICK M. JONES - INVENTOR OF REFRIGERATION EQUIPMENT AND MORE

Frederick M. Jones was born on May 17, 1893 in Covington, Kentucky on the South Bank of the Ohio River and was an inquisitive child. After reaching adulthood, Frederick McKinley Jones is credited with more than 60 patents, 40 of which are for refrigeration equipment alone. His first interest was in auto mechanics and racing cars. After serving as an electrician in World War I, Jones moved into radio and movie electronics and developed motion picture equipment and a ticket dispensing machine.

By the 1930s, Jones was designing portable air-cooling units for trucks that transported perishable foods. His company also manufactured refrigeration units for trains, ships and planes. Jones was the recognized authority on refrigeration engineering and on December 7, 1954 became the first African American member of the American Society of Engineers.

Frederick McKinley Jones is responsible for the way we receive our food from farmers across the nation. On February 21, 1961 Frederick McKinley Jones died from lung cancer at the age of 68, and buried at Fort Snelling as a Veteran of World War I.

HERMON L. GRIMES
INVENTOR OF FOLDING WING AIRCRAFT

Hermon L. Grimes in 1936 received a patent as the inventor of Folding Wing Aircraft that was used in combat for takeoff on aircraft carriers. Folding aircraft enabled the U.S. Navy to stock more planes on its aircraft carriers and gave the U.S. an advantage over Japanese carriers. Folding Wing Aircraft such as Hell Cat, Tiger Cat and Wild Cat accounted for over 75 percent of the downed enemy aircraft in the Pacific Theatre.

The invention of Folding Wing Aircraft shortened World War II and saved many American lives. It was the forerunner to the modern technology which is presently used in the designing of fighter aircraft. President George Bush flew the Avenger Bomber, also a Folding Wing Aircraft during World War II.

As an African American, Grimes never received recognition for or a penny for this invention and died frustrated by the fact that his invention was so useful but he was not recognized nor was he able to leave any compensation to his heirs. His family is now striving to correct history books dealing with the subjects of aircraft and World War II.

ANN MOORE AND THE SNUGLI

Ann Moore and her husband worked as Peace Corps volunteers in the early 1960's. As a pediatric nurse in Africa, Ann saw lots of mothers and babies every day and noticed the contentment of the babies as they spent long hours snuggled up happily in fabric harnesses against their mothers' backs. Two months after her return to the United States, Ann gave birth to a baby girl and wanted the same closeness with her child. She developed a fabric pouch to carry her daughter snugly on her back, and even accompanied Martin Luther King on his famous march from Selma to Montgomery.

Working with her mother, an experienced seamstress, she improved the design calling it the "SNUGLI". People who saw Ann Moore walking with her baby began to order and by 1972 orders for 300 Snuglis a month were pouring in. After the highest ranking reviews by Consumer Report and the Wall Street Journal, sales hit the $6 Million mark. The business remained a family operation until 1985 when Gerico bought the patent.

Ann Moore also invented the "Airlift", a padded, portable and adjustable oxygen carrier. This backpack gives greater freedom to people who need a steady supply of oxygen. She also designed a shoulder/hand bag and carrier to fit on the back of a wheelchair or walker.

LONNIE JOHNSON
INVENTOR OF THE SUPER SOAKER

Lonnie Johnson has been creating toys for the past 40 years. As a teenager he won first place in a National Collegiate Competition for his invention "LINEX", a remote controlled robot. He later attended Tuskeegee University on a math scholarship and was elected to the National Engineering Honor Society. He graduated with distinction with a Bachelors Degree in Mechanical Engineering and completed a Masters Degree in Nuclear Engineering two years later.

While a captain in the Air Force, he was awarded the Air Force Achievement Medal and received the Air Force Commendation Medal twice. As a Spacecraft Systems Engineer for Jet Propulsion Laboratory (JPL), he worked on the Galileo and Mars Observer Projects while simultaneously pursuing his inventions. In 1985, he formed the Lonnie G. Johnson Engineering Company. Six years later, he expanded and renamed his company Johnson Research & Development Company to include a design and marketing division.

Lonnie Johnson holds over 23 patents and received the patent for the world's most successful water gun the "Super Soaker" on December 24, 1991.

MORRIS B. WILLIAMS - INVENTOR RESTORATION OF THE STATUE OF LIBERTY

The French artist Bartholdi originally designed the Statue of Liberty as France's tribute to the Emancipation of the United States slaves. The statue had African features and the broken chains of slavery hanging from her arms. When the United States government received the statue, Bartholdi was encouraged to alter the image to what we see today.

But how ironic when the country celebrated the 100th birthday of the Statue of Liberty, it was Morris B. Williams, an African American from New York City, while working for Amsterdam Colorworks, who developed a Polymeric Water-Reducible Paint to restore the Statue. Williams is recognized among New York area paint technologists as one of the most innovative paint chemists in the business.

As one of the few Black Technical directors in the industry, the product used on the Statue was tested for six months by engineers of Lehr-McGovern Corp. in charge of the renovation project. The Diamonite product was declared the coating of choice and also approved for use to restore the Statue. With the use of the paint developed by Morris B. Williams, the Statue of Liberty is now ready for the next 100 years.

NTESIE

"Would America have been America without her Negro people."
—W.E.B. DuBois

BI-NKA-BI

SYMBOLIZES: ***JUSTICE, FAIR PLAY AND FREEDOM***

CHAPTER NINE

1. CARTER G. WOODSON
2. FIRST AFRICAN AMERICAN LIBRARY
3. FORTY ACRES AND A MULE -
   WHAT HAPPENED?
4. SLAVERY - THE ALAMO -
   AND THE YELLOW ROSE OF TEXAS
5. JUNETEENTH
6. NANCY GREEN
7. THE PROMISE OF FREEDOM /
   FIRST AFRICAN CONVERSION TO
   AMERICAN CHRISTIANITY
8. BEHIND THE FOURTH OF JULY

CARTER G. WOODSON FATHER OF BLACK HISTORY MONTH

Carter G. Woodson - Father of Black History month was born on December 19, 1875 in New Canton, Virginia and is known as the Father of Black History Month.

Carter G. Woodson whose parents were former slaves went to work in a coal-mine at the age of 17, and by the age of 18 received a diploma. Woodson later went on to become a principal of the school where he graduated. He received a Ph.D in history from Harvard University and a Spingarn Medal in 1926 from the NAACP. He was an African American dedicated to preserving the records of Black People.

Dr. Woodson recognized the need for recording the history of Black people in 1915 and devoted his life to bringing the accomplishments of African Americans to the World's attention when he started the trend that gathered momentum during the Civil Rights Movement.

Dr. Woodson founded the Association for the Study of Afro-American Life and History and began publishing scholarly material. Currently, the most familiar publications and best known of Dr. Woodson's 16 books is the "MISEDUCATION OF THE NEGRO" and the "EDUCATION OF THE NEGRO".

Dr. Carter G. Woodson founded Black History Week which is now Black History Month and soon it will be everyday. Dr. Carter G. Woodson - the recorder of Black history and Father of Black History Month.

FIRST AFRICAN AMERICAN LIBRARY

One of the Nation's first public libraries was launched on February 20, 1833 with the founding of the Philadelphia Library Company of Colored Persons. The Founders advanced a tradition of African reading and writing over two thousand years old. When African nations were conquered during the enslavement process, among the first people killed were the scholars and those entrusted with the keys of Knowledge.

The oral historians known as Griots who survived were able to decode the ghostly writings on surfaces that the conquerors had not destroyed - Pyramid Walls, Sealed Temples, Caves and Ancient Tablets. These ancient writings revealed that the tradition of African libraries dates back to that of Egypt's King Osymandyas, Circa 1240 B.C. and much of what is known as "Greek Philosophy" was derived from the ancient religious system known as the "Egyptian Mysteries". The first African American library founded in Philadelphia empowered the African American through knowledge and in the words of an Egyptian inscription - "KNOW THYSELF".

WHAT HAPPENED TO THE FORTY ACRES AND A MULE? SPECIAL FIELD ORDER #15

The "Forty Acres and a Mule". What happened to it?

On January 12, 1865, in the midst of his "March to the Sea" during the Civil War, General William T. Sherman and Secretary of War, Edwin M. Stanton met with 20 Black community leaders of Savannah, Georgia. Based, in part, to their input, Gen. Sherman's Special Field Order #15 on January 16, 1865 was to set aside the Sea Islands and a 30 mile inland tract of land starting along the Southern Coast of Charleston and extending down to the St. John River, Florida, for the exclusive settlement of Blacks. Each family would receive 40 acres of land and an army mule to work the land, thus "Forty Acres and a Mule".

Gen. Rufus Saxton was assigned by Sherman to implement the order. On a national level, this and other land, confiscated and abandoned, became the jurisdiction of the Freedman's Bureau, which was headed by Gen. Oliver Otis Howard, (Founder of Howard University). In his words he wanted to "Give the Freedmen protection, land and schools as far and as fast as he can."

However, during the summer and fall of 1865, President Andrew Johnson issued special pardons, returning the property to the Ex-Confederates. Howard issued Circular 13, giving 40 acres as quickly as possible. Upon his knowledge, President Johnson ordered Howard to issue Circular 15, returning the land to the original slave holders.

THE YELLOW ROSE OF TEXAS SLAVERY AND THE ALAMO

The story of "The Sweetest Little Rosebud" described in the Texas State Anthem, "The Yellow Rose of Texas" was inspired by the story of Emily, a Black Woman and slave who changed the history of Texas. In March 1836 Texas declared itself independent of Mexico and a Republic in its own right to **preserve slavery** in the State of Texas. The Alamo, a century old Spanish Mission, became the proving ground where the armies of Mexico and Texas battled for control and the continuation of slavery in the State of Texas.

After winning the first round of fighting in March, Texas struck back in the Battle of San Jacinto. Santa Anna's 1,500 man army was caught off guard and because their leader, General Santa Anna was preoccupied. The General was nowhere to be found until the next day, April 22, 1836, when it was revealed that he had been with Emily, an enslaved Black woman.

Emily had done Texas a big favor and the people began to sing "She's the sweetest little rosebud that Texas ever knew". And as they sing the song "The Yellow Rose of Texas is the Only Girl for Me" they give tribute to an African American woman who unknowingly distracted Santa Anna in one of the Battles of Texas and its quest to maintain slavery as a way of life for people of African heritage.

JUNETEENTH
THE TEXAS HOLIDAY

What is the history of Juneteenth?

Each year on June 19th, descendants of enslaved human beings in the United States gather for the first official Black holiday celebrating the day in 1865 when General Gordon Granger and his troops arrived in Galveston, Texas to re-enforce Abraham Lincoln's Emancipation Proclamation. Major General Granger was ordered to Texas from New Orleans on June 10, 1865, bringing with him three proclamations aimed at the lawful restructure of the government of Texas more than two and a half years after Lincoln issued the Proclamation in 1863.

By 1865, the Proclamation had freed more than 200,000 slaves. Most Black slaves knew of the Emancipation through newspapers, letters and word of mouth, but ten days after Major Granger landed in Galveston, on June 20, 1865, The Galveston News became the first newspaper to report that as of June 19, 1865 the slaves in Texas were to be set free, which was the legal end to slavery in Texas. Even with the Emancipation Proclamation in force, slaves around the United States were not truly free until the 13th Amendment to the Constitution was passed.

As the first official Black holiday, the celebration of Juneteenth is a significant event in history celebrated in over 200 cities throughout the United States as a part of our heritage.

NANCY GREEN
THE ORIGINAL AUNT JEMIMA

Nancy Green was born into slavery in Montgomery County, Kentucky in 1831. At the age of 15, she became an apprentice cook and was considered fortunate to learn how to cook many foods that were both French and American from a chef who had special training in France.

After the Civil War, she settled in Chicago and found a job as a cook in the home of a prominent Chicago judge. The life of Aunt Jemima began when Chris L. Rutt, a newspaperman, and Charles G. Underwood invested in the Pearl Milling Co. in Missouri in 1889 and were searching for a way to survive in the highly competitive flour business. After attending a minstrel show, Mr. Rutt heard a catchy tune called "Aunt Jemima" sung by a black-faced performer clad in an apron and bandanna head wrap. After working on the "Aunt Jemima Recipe" for a year without capital, Rutt and Underwood sold out to R.T. Davis Milling Co.

Mr. Davis, enjoying the cooking of Black slave women during years of slavery, decided to actually employ a Black woman as a living trademark for his "Aunt Jemima Recipe". He was introduced to Nancy Green who was a storyteller, singer and excellent cook. He signed Nancy to a lifetime contract and she made her debut as the "Original Aunt Jemima" at the Chicago's World Fair in 1893. Nancy cooked pancakes outside the Davis Exhibit while she sang and told stories.

Nancy Green's expertise in making pancakes on the griddle became the advertising world's first living trademark, a national celebrity and the true reason for the success of the institution known as "Aunt Jemima's Pancakes".

FIRST AFRICAN CONVERSION TO AMERICAN CHRISTIANITY THE PROMISE OF FREEDOM

The first Africans brought to colonial Jamestown in 1619 were called "Indentures", the same term used for whites working off prison time, debt, apprenticeship or Transatlantic Passage with years of servitude. The white planters learned that the benefit of Black Indentures was that their skin color prevented them from escaping or disappearing into the general white population.

The Virginia Court records from the early 17th Century indicate that as the African Indentures neared the end of their five to seven year term, they petitioned the Courts for their freedom. The judges granted the wealthy planters free labor by creating a crime - Africans were found guilty of heathenism, which was punishable by extended servitude.

Africans began to avoid punishment by converting to American Christianity and leaving the ways of their spirituality of Africa. They began to baptize their newborn babies so they would not be indentures.

By January 1626, nearly seven years after the first boatload had landed, the converted Africans were promised freedom for which they worked but never received.

BEHIND THE FOURTH OF JULY - THE MASONS AND THE DECLARATION OF INDEPENDENCE

The Declaration of Independence adopted by the Second Continental Congress on July 4, 1776 led to the establishment of the United States of America. But the founding fathers were influenced by the philosophical ideologies of the Secret Societies in France, Germany and England. Fifty of the 56 signers of the Declaration were active members in various Masonic organizations.

These men of the Masonic organizations were believers that Ancient Egypt was the birthplace of Masonry and the Nile Valley teachings of measurements and proportions were used in buildings which were designed to represent the Universe and man's relationship to it and symbolized God as the "Master Architect".

In the creation of the United States, the founding fathers wanted to recreate the spiritual essence that once existed in the Nile Valley. As Masons in writing the Declaration of Independence, the founding fathers were actually influenced by the history and writings of Ancient Egypt (known as Kemet).

BI-NKA-BI

"There is a debt to the Negro people
which America can never repay.
At least then, they must make amends."
—SOJOURNER TRUTH

PEMPAMSIE

SYMBOLIZES: ***SUGGESTING NEED FOR EVER READINESS, STEADFASTNESS, HARDINESS, VALOR AND FEARLESSNESS***

CHAPTER TEN

1. KENTE CLOTH
2. THE THANKSGIVING TURKEY
3. HISTORY OF THE DOZENS
4. ORIGIN OF THE WORD "CRACKERS
5. ORIGIN OF THE WORD "COWBOY"
6. ORIGIN OF THE WORD "BAR-B-Q"
7. THE ORIGIN OF THE WORD "SLAVE" AND "SLAVERY"
8. THE MAMELUKES

KENTE CLOTH - ITS ORIGIN, ITS HISTORY

The history of Ghana's Kente cloth began during Africa's colonization by Europe after the Berlin Conference in 1817. The European colonizers "owned" the natural raw resources grown by Africans and when harvested were taken to be manufactured in European factories and sold back to the African at extremely high prices.

When the "Gold Coast" took its independence in 1957 as "Ghana", the newly elected President Kwame Nkrumah knew that his nation's ability to take control of its resources, manufacturing and production of marketable assets was critical to Ghana's future. Nkrumah revived a rich long tradition of art and textiles to symbolize Ghana's ability to profit by its own hands and the industry of the weaving of the cloth traditionally worn by Ghanaian royalty woven with distinctive patterns preserved for centuries.

Knowing the historical background of this royal cloth, African Americans should not tolerate the poor quality imitations of the Kente pattern coming to the United States - but not from Ghana. Preserve African history — Demand authentic Kente cloth.

THE ORIGIN OF THE THANKSGIVING TURKEY

The origin of the turkey eaten at the Thanksgiving table was called the "Guinea-Fowl" from Guinea, West Africa which was brought into Europe through the country, Turkey. According to the book "THE STORY OF MANKIND" by Hendrik William Van Loon who wrote that an "African from Egypt travelled to Europe where he taught Europeans civilization which included speech and writing...".

The first "turkey" eaten by the Europeans was the Guinea Fowl. The word "Guinea Fowl" was kept for what was known as the old world of Europe and the "Turkey" word was used by the early settlers when they arrived in America. They saw a wild fowl that reminded them of the turkey-cocks and turkey-hens that they had seen in turkey which was actually named after the Guinea Fowl from Africa. The pilgrims then named the strange American fowl "turkeys" and the name appears as early as 1607 in writings of Captain John Smith.

Later it was discovered that the American variety that we call "turkey" was an entirely different species. It is the first cousin of the buzzard which is an american vulture of the hawk family of fowls.

THE HISTORY OF THE DOZENS

When slave auctioneers had "exceptional" merchandise - human beings sold into slavery, they would sell African people as individuals separately. When they thought the "Items" (African Individuals) were flawed in some way - age, illnesses, deformities, they would then sell them in lots, most times in dozens. Every slave knew that if he was included among the dozens, that something was physically wrong with him or her. It was also considered humiliating to be a part of a "dozen".

Eventually, as time passed, the term was applied to a ritualized verbal battle that Black people developed to insult and humiliate each other. The focus was on genealogy and the point is total humiliation. The loser was the one, who because his emotions took control or because his insults were too weak, took refuge in physical abuse. The winner was the one with the cruelest insult who managed to keep his cool. The history of the dozens - from the slave trade.

ORIGIN OF THE WORD "CRACKERS"

During the period of 1600 to 1769, several books in history indicate that many of the early settlers were descendents from convicts that were transported from Great Britain to Virginia at different times and inherited so much immortality from their ancestors that they were considered the most abandoned set of men on earth; according to Chief Justice Stokes of the Colony of Georgia during that time.

In 1753 Benjamin Franklin complained that English and German jails were being emptied into America and considered it an insult and threatended to send King George a cargo of rattlesnakes in return.

Chief Justice Stokes of the Colony of Georgia during that same time also wrote "The Southern colonies are overrun with a swarm of men from the Eastern parts of Virginia and North Carolina, distinguished by the name of "Crackers".

Thus, the origin of the Word "Crackers" from Chief Justice Stokes in 1753.

ORIGIN OF THE WORD THE COWBOY AND THE RODEO

Florida once included parts of Louisiana, Mississippi and Alabama, wherein slave owners would march their slaves into Texas to avoid the clouds of the Civil War.

With that, instead of cotton, some Blacks gathered stray cattle called "Mavericks", after a rancher would abandon the effort. When the trails were opened to drive cattle to Chicago for the Urban cities of the East, the planter or farmer became "Cattlemen", and the Black man a "Cow Boy".

During the early years of Rodeo, Black Cattlemen and Black Cowboys made very little effort to take their talents and commercialize their skills, but they frequently competed as amateurs. They were always outdoing each other, and there were always Black Cowboys who loved to try and rope any steer or ride any bronco just for the hell of it. In 1884, a Black Cowboy in Mobeetie, Texas, broke the record for roping, throwing and tying steers in one minute and thirteen seconds. By 1887, there were cowboys like "Pinto Jim" and "Bronco Jim Davis" who were an active part of the birth of the Rodeo.

It was discrimination and the lack of money that kept the Black Cowboy from participating in the Rodeo but they were there from the beginning. One of the grandest Rodeos was held in Madison Square Garden in New York, and considered one of the all time greats because people had come to see Bill Pickett's act, of taking down the steer by biting its upper lip and making it helpless. But his steer had become unruly and agitated by the crowd, and got the jump on Bill Pickett's horse. The steer jumped the gate and landed in the grandstand. Pickett went after the steer and jumped the gate with the intent to bulldog the steer in the grandstand. Bill rode the steer down, bulldogged it right there while Will Rogers, who was also in the act, assisted by picking the steer up by the heels and Pickett hung on the horns and dragged the animal back to the arena. The newspaper coverage packed Madison Garden for the remainder of the performances. The Black Cowboy and the Rodeo - there from the start.

THE ORIGIN OF THE WORD BAR-B-Q

South Florida was a haven for Black people in flight from slavery as far back as the 17th Century. Many escaped from plantations of the South and intermarried with local native Americans, who were exiled from the Creek areas of the Carolinas and they took the name Seminole meaning "Runaway".

At the end of the American War of Independence, the British evacuated Charleston and Savannah and took approximately 8,300 former slaves to South Florida. Upset and wanting to reclaim their human property, Southern slaveholders engaged in the Seminole Wars to return the runaway slaves back to the plantations. American slave hunters repeatedly raided the State of Florida for Runaways.

The Maroon, African People who lived among the Indians, and working with the Indians, resisted the troops of the United States of Slavery. The Timucuan Indians practiced a form of torture where the victim was turned slowly over smoldering embers which was called BAR-B-Q originating from the Spanish word "Barbacoa". In retaliation for war crimes, it was also used by Maroons and Indians against captured soldiers.

THE ORIGIN OF THE WORD SLAVE AND SLAVERY

The word "SLAVE" was originally applied to white people. It comes from "Slav", a Russian people captured by the Germans. The first slaves held in the United States were not Black, but white, who were mostly Europeans from Britain. In Virginia, white servitude was for a limited period of time, but was sometimes extended for life. In the West Indies, it was extended for life for Irish people.

White people were sold in the United States up to 1826, fifty years after the signing of the Declaration of Independence. Andrew Johnson, President of the United States, was a runaway, and was advertised for in the newspaper.

White children were kidnapped at the rate of several thousand yearly in the 17th and 18th centuries and sold into slavery in America and the West Indies. They were bootlegged and sold as "Negroes". White Americans, North and South, were also kidnapped and deduced and sold as Negroes as late as 1859. One of the most celebrated cases of a white person sold as a Negro was Sally Muller, who was held in servitude in Louisiana for 26 years. Court after court ruled against her, and finally her birth certificate was found in Germany and she was freed by the Supreme Court in 1818.

THE MAMELUKES AND THE GREAT LEAP

The Mamelukes was a dynasty of slaves who ruled Egypt more than 600 years. Most of them were white slaves from Russia and Armenia, but many were Africans from the Sudan. Mohammed Ali, a Macedonian-born Mercenary, only concerned with selling the riches of Egypt to the highest bidder in 1811 put an end to their power. He summoned them all to Cairo pretending to be consulting with them concerning an invasion of Arabia and invited them to a great feast in his honor.

After a hospitable reception they were invited to parade in the courtyard, and as they did so the walls closed behind them and immediately the army of Mohammed Ali opened fire, ambushed and murdered in a barrage of rifle and cannon fire upon the defenseless men but the Mamelukes met death worthy of their past deeds of valor.

Only one escaped to tell the manner of his companions death. He spurred his horse and without dismounting, horse and rider leaped over the walls making a leap which has never been outdone in all history. He freed himself from the dying horse and escaped into the desert as a hero, taking the great leap of the Mameluke to freedom.

PEMPAMSIE

"History is a clock that people use to tell their time of day.
It is a compass they use to find themselves
on a map of Human Geography.
It tells them where , they are,
and what they are."
—John Henrik Clarke

NYAMEDUA

SYMBOLIZES: *GOD'S PRESENCE EVERYWHERE AND EVERY TIME.*

CHAPTER ELEVEN

1. PINCKNEY BENTON STEWART PINCHBACK
   - GOVERNOR FOR 35 DAYS
2. DR. PATRICIA BATH
   - INVENTOR OF THE CATARACT LASERPHACOPROBE

Tom Joyner's Favorite "Little Known Black History Fact"

PINCKNEY BENTON STEWART PINCHBACK - GOVERNOR FOR 35 DAYS

PINCKNEY BENTON STEWART PINCHBACK at the age of 12 years old took a job as a cabin boy on a riverboat and worked on the Mississippi and Missouri Rivers until he was 25; he moved to Louisiana and served in the army and then settled in New Orleans. Pinchback became involved in politics and served as Lieutenant Governor of the State of Louisiana.

On December 9, 1872, P.B.S. Pinchback became Governor but did not have much time to do the job. During the Reconstruction Period there were many Black elected officials but they were removed from office by fraud, terror or political manuevering because white politicians feared and used propaganda threats of Black domination. That is what happened to P.B.S. Pinchback in 1871. As a prominent publisher of the NEW ORLEANS LOUISIANIAN, he was elected President Pro Tempore of the State Senate. However, when the Lieutenant Governor died, Pinchback by constitutional order filled the post. But when the Governor was suspended under threat of impeachment a year later, Pinchback became Acting Governor. Even after having support for his position as Governor, it was suggested to him that it would be *"best"* if he withdrew gracefully and that he would be appointed to a six-year term in the U.S. Senate. This arrangment was not honored and Pinchback was denied the Senate seat, but he was voted the equivalent of his salary for the equivalent time period. P.B.S. Pinchback experienced one of the first and many injustices in the political arena.

LADY SALA S. SHABAZZ'S
FAVORITE
"LITTLE KNOWN BLACK HISTORY FACT"

DR. PATRICIA BATH
INVENTOR OF THE CATARACT LASERPHACOPROBE

PATRICIA BATH, M.D., is the inventor of the cataract Laserphacoprobe, which is the medical instument to remove cataracts from the eye. Dr. Bath was the first Black Female Surgeon appointed to UCLA in 1975, and is credited with the founding of the Student National Medical Association along with other Howard University Students; and, was its first president. Together with associates and colleagues founded the American Institute for the Prevention of Blindness and with limited funding provided free vision screening services to underserved communities.

Dr. Bath holds several other firsts: First African American woman surgeon at Drew Medical School; First Woman Program Director (Chief) of a Postgraduate training program at Drew; First Woman Chair of Opthalmology in the History of the United States form 1983-1986, Drew-UCLA Residency program; First Woman Faculty Opthalmologist of UCLA Dept. of Opthalmology, Jules Stein Eye Institute with her appointment in 1975; First Woman elected to Honorary Medical Staff of UCLA Medical Center upon her Retirement in 1993; Elected to Hunter College Hall of Fame in 1988 and Elected as Howard University Pioneer in Academic Medicine in 1993.

As the first African American female physician/inventor, Dr. Bath, in the early part of her career devoted herself to the prevention of blindness in the United States and Internationally. Her intense interest, experience and research on cataracts culminated in 1985-1986 with her invention of a new device and method to remove cataracts. With this invention, Dr. Patricia Bath was able to recover the sight of several individuals who had been blind for over 30 years. As a laser scientist and inventor, Dr. Bath has four patents on a laser cataract surgery device covering the United States, Canada, Japan and Europe.

NYAMEDUA

"I call gold,
gold is mute.
I call cloth,
cloth is mute.
It is mankind that matters"
—*Unknown - Akan of West Africa*

ADINKRA SYMBOL EXPLANATIONS PER CHAPTER

OPENING ONE:

GYE NYAME: ONLY GOD

The symbol depicts the belief in the supremacy of God and signifies God's omnipotence, omnipresence and omniscience. God has power over everything and everyone.

CHAPTER ONE

SANKOFA: RETURN AND PICK IT UP

Learn from or build on the past. Pick up the gems of the past. A constant reminder that the past is not all shameful and that the future may profitably be built on aspects of the past.

CHAPTER TWO

BESA SAKA: BUNCH OF COLA NUTS

Symbolizes Affulence and Power.

CHAPTER THREE

NKYINKYIMIE: TWISTINGS

The symbol depicts toughness and selfless devotion to service and the ability to withstand difficulties.

CHAPTER FOUR

DAMEDAME

Symbolizes craftiness and intelligence.

CHAPTER FIVE

DWENNINMEN: RAM'S HEAD

The symbol of humility and strength, wisdom and learning.

CHAPTER SIX

AYA: FERN

Symbol of endurance and defiance of difficulties.

CHAPTER SEVEN

HWEMUDUA: MEASURING ROD

The symbol of the belief in the best that can be of everything and there is no tolerance of imperfection.

CHAPTER EIGHT

NTESIE

Symbolizes wisdom, knowledge and prudence.

CHAPTER NINE

BI-NKA-BI

Symbolic of justice, fair play and freedom.

CHAPTER TEN

PEMPAMSIE

Symbolic suggesting need for ever readiness, steadfastness, hardiness, valor and fearlessness.

CHAPTER ELEVEN

NYAMEDUA

Symbolizes God's presence everywhere and every time.

BIBLIOGRAPHY AND LIST OF REFERENCES

REFERENCES

Nile Valley Contributions to Civilization - Exploding the Myths Volume 1
By Anthony T. Browder
The Institute of Karmic Guidance
Washington, D.C. 20056
Copyright 1992

The Black Book
By Middleton Harris
Random House, New York
Copyright 1994

Blacks in Science
Astrophysicist to Zoologist
By Hatti Carwell
Self Published
Copyright 1977

Black Women In Antiquity
Edited by Ivan Van Sertima
Transaction Books, New Brunswick and London
Copyright 1994 by Journal of African Civilizations Ltd., Inc.

Ancient Egyptian Survivals in the Pacific
By R. A. Jairazbhoy
Published by Carnac House
Copyright 1990

Salute to Black Women
By Black Science Activity Books Learning Activities
Published by Chandler/White Puclishing Company,
Chicago, Illinois
Copyright 1990

The Colored Inventor
By Henry E. Baker
Ayer Company Publishers, Inc.
Salem, New Hampshire

Black Women for Beginners
A writers and Readers Beginners Documentary Comic Book
Black Studies Series
Women's Study Series

Blacks in Science
Ancient and Modern
Editor: Ivan Van Sertima
Transaction Books, New Brunswick and London
Copyright 1983 The Journal of African Civilization Limited, Inc.

Black Inventors from Africa to America
Two Millon Years of Invention and Innovation
By C. R. Gibbs
Three Dimensional Publishing Co.,
Silver Springs, Maryland
Copyright 1995

Black Heritage Day II
By Carl Bernard Mack
Engineer, Author, Lecturer, Actor
(Desktop Calendar)

Black Women Makers of History - A Portrait
By George F. Jackson
Copyright 1975 by G.F. Jackson

Black Contributors to Science and Energy Technology
Published by the U.S. Department of Energy
Office of Public Affairs
Washington, D.C.

1001 Black Inventions Supplement
Written and Researched by
Ersky Freeman
Editor: Alayo E. Moseley
Pin Point, Inc.
Copyright 1991

American Slavery
1619 to 1877
By Peter Kolchin
Published by Hill & Wang,
New York
Copyright 1990

I've Got an Idea
A Story of Frederick McKinley Jones
By Gloria M. Swanson
and Margaret V. Ott
Runstone Press, Minneapolis
Copyright 1994

Ebony
A Johnson Publication
The Bicentennial: 200 Years of Black Trails and Triumphs
Special Issue
August 1975

Newsweek
January 11, 1988
The Search for Adam and Eve
Scientists Explore a Controversial Theory About Man's Origin
Newsweek, Inc.
New York, New York

U.S. News
A Stunning New Discovery in Egypt's Valley of the Kings
Tales from the Crypt
May 29, 1995

Black History is No Mystery
Volume 1 of 1
By William M. Singleton, Jr.
Published by Quest Company
Boston, Mass.

Nine African American Inventors
By Robert C. Hayden
Published by 21st Century Books
Frederick, Maryland
Copyright 1972

A Pictorial History of the Slave Trade
By Minerva
Copyright 1971

Glory Days
365 Inspired Moments in African-American History
By Janice Adams
Harper Collins,
New York, New York
Copyright 1995

Ebony
A Johnson Publication
The First Generation
The Birth of Black America
By Lerone Bennett, Jr.,
June 1969
The Legacy of My Husband Malcolm X
By Betty Shabazz

Newsweek
February 13, 1995
What Color is Black?
Science, Politics and Racial Identity
Newsweek, Inc.
New York, New York

Time Magazine
May 29, 1995
Secrets of the Lost Tomb
The Discovery of a Crypt Fit for 50 Princes, Sheds New Light on the Epic Life of Rameses the Great

Black History is No Mystery Volume No. 2
Winter 1993-1994
Publisher and Editor William M. Singleton, Jr., Quest Magazine Communications, Inc.
Copyright 1993

YSB
The Magazine for Young Sisters and Brothers
Page Publications, Inc.
Copyright January 1994

Class
The Most Comprehensive Black Magazine
R-E John-Sandy Communications, Ltd., New York, New York
Copyright September 1993

Class
Black Music Month
R-E John-Sandy Communications, Ltd., New York, New York
Copyright June 1994

Egypt's Pyramids: Houses of Eternity
Teachers' Guide
National Geographic Society
Washington, D.C.
Copyright 1978

Black Achievers In Science
Museum of Science and Industry
Chicago, Illinois
Copyright 1988

Black History is No Mystery Volume 1 No. 2
Publisher and Editor William M. Singleton, Jr., Quest Magazine Communications, Inc.
Boston, Mass
Copyright 1993

American Way
December 15, 1994
American Airlines/American Eagle

Class
The Most Comprehensive Black Magazine
R-E John-Sandy Communications, Ltd., New York, New York
Copyright July and August 1993

Class
Black History Month 1994
R-E John-Sandy Communications, Ltd., New York, New York
Copyright 1994 Issue

The National Inventors Hall of Fame
1994 National Inventors Hall of Fame

Life World Library
Tropical Africa
Life World Library
Time Incorporated, New York
Copyright 1962

Eleven African American Doctors
Achievers: African Americans in Science and Technology
By Robery C. Hayden
21st Century Books
Frederick, Maryland
Copyright 1976

Seven African American Scientists
By Robert C. Hayden
21st Century Books
Frederick, Maryland
Copyright 1970

Benjamin Banneker
Scientist and Mathematician
By Kevin Connolly
Chelsea House Publishers
New York and Philadelphia
Copyright 1989

Black Wallstreet
By Jay Jay Wilson and Ron Wallace
Black Wallstreet Publishing Co.
Tulsa, Oklahoma
Copyright 1992

Many Pictorial Gems of Blacks National and International
from the Scrapbook of Alfred Grumbles, Jr.
HRP Enterprise
Memphis, Tennessee
Copyright 1972

Corners of Black History
By Reginald Larrie
King Company
Detroit, MI
Copyright 1971

We Florida
A Publication of the Florida Black Historical Research Project
By Isa Hamm Bryant
Copyright 1996

100 Amazing Facts About the Negro With Complete Proof
By J. A. Rogers
Published by Helga M. Rogers
St. Petersburg, Florida
Copyright 1957, 1995

African American Firsts
Famous Little Known and Unsung Triumphs of Blacks in America
By Joan Potter
with Constance Clothier
Pinto Press
Elizabethtown, New York
Copyright 1994

Africa's Gift to America
By J. A. Rogers
Published by Helda M. Rogers
St. Petersburg, Florida
Copyright 1957

African American Times
A Chronological Record
An Impact "Black History" Publication
Impact Publishing Company
Copyright 1991

Before the Mayflower
a History of Black America
By Lerone Bennett, Jr.
Penguin Books
New York, NY
Copyright 1962, 1969, and 1988

50 Unknown Facts About the African With Complete Proof
By Dr. G.K. Osei
No. 1 of the African Empire Study Booklet A.P.S.
The African Publication Society
London England
Copyright 1964

The Ancient Black Christians
By Father Martin DePorres Walsh, OP.
Julian Richardson & Associates
Publishers, San Francisco, CA

The Children of the Sun
By George Wyles Parker
Black Classic Press
Baltimore, Maryland

Timbuktu Afrovision
By Daud Malik Watts
Positive Image Education Series
Volume 1, No. 2
Afrovision, Inc.
Copyright 1986

Ebony Pictorial History of Black America
Volume I - IV
By the Editors of Ebony
Johnson Publishing Company, Inc.
Chicago, Illinois
Copyright 1971

Valerie J. Robinson

LADY SALA S. SHABAZZ (Valerie J. Robinson) was born in Harlem Hospital, New York and raised in Jersey City, New Jersey. After moving to Los Angeles, California in 1976, Lady Sala continued her studies in African and African American history, including traveling internationally to countries: England; Egypt; Senegal; The Gambia; Bahia and Rio de Janario, Brazil; Belize, Central America; Ghana-West / Africa and, several Caribbean countries: Nassau, Jamaica, Freeport, Barbados, Trinidad, Turks & Caicos Islands and St. Lucia.

Honors include Who's Who In Executive and Professional Women, The Book of Honor for Community Service and The International Who's Who of Intellectuals. Awards received from The International Conference of Women as a "Anyhow Woman" in Bahia, Brazil; and Passages to Success Award, in Los Angeles.

She has received Commendations from the cities of Compton, California; Muskogee, Oklahoma; Detroit, Michigan; Chicago, Illinois, the Key to the City of Baton Rouge, Louisiana; and, San Bernardino, California.

Tom Joyner, The Fly Jock

I first recall meeting Lady Sala Shabazz at the Congressional Black Caucus in D.C. I visited her display that included a room full of gadgets invented by Black people. I was impressed. Like so many African Americans, I was familiar with the contributions of George Washington Carver and Charles Drew. But what Lady Sala offered took things to another level.

I had just launched a national radio show heard in several cities around the country and I thought it would be a great idea for Lady Sala to share some of her vast knowledge during Black History Month. Intrigued by her depth and her "fineness," I gave her a call when I returned to Dallas. She liked the idea and then I thought, why stop with Black History Month in February. There is enough little known information about black people to fill every day of the year. " Hey, Lady Sala," I said, "Can you hook a brother up?"

She agreed, but only if I would promise to make a contriution to her museum in Los Angeles.

So, we worked something out. But before we made our deal, Lady Sala wanted to know a few facts about me. I told her how I once had a morning radio show in Dallas and an afternoon radio show in Chicago and commuted back and forth from the two cities daily for eight years. In 1997 the Tom Joyner Morning Show went national and is currently heard by satellite in close to one hundred cities including Los Angeles, Dallas, Chicago, Philly, Atlanta, Miami and D.C., just to name a few. Each morning nearly five million listeners tune in. And thanks to Lady Sala, the Little Known Black History Facts is one of the most popular features on the Tom Joyner Morning Show. After four years, I'm still finding out things I never know about Black people, and I look forward to many more years of working with Lady Sala. As long as Black people are making contributions, Lady Sala will be searching them out and bringing them to the forefront, and that's a fact.

SUGGESTED READING

Blacks in Science
Nile Valley Civilizations
They Came Before Columbus
Black Women In Antiquity .... Author: *Ivan Van Sertima*

Black Man of the Nile and His Family
Africa — Mother of Western Civilization .... Author: *Yosef ben-Jochannan*

Africa's Gift to America .... Author: *J.A. Rogers*

The African Contribution .... Author: *John M. Weatherwax*

Black Inventors of America .... Author: *McKinley Burt, Jr.*

The Destruction of Black Civilization .... Author: *Chancellor Williams*

The Black Book .... Author: *Middleton Harris*

Before the Mayflower .... Author: *Lerone Bennett, Jr.*

Glory Days - 365 Inspired Moments
In African American History .... Author: *Janice Adams*

The Real McCoy: African American
Invention and Innovation .... Author: *Portia P. James*

Also

Visit your local African American bookstore
for additional publications not listed here.

OTHER PUBLICATIONS OF SALA ENTERPRISES

THE KWANZAA COLORING BOOK $5.95

Copyright 1985

First comprehensive, yet simple explanation of the celebration of Kwanzaa for children of all ages. Not only a coloring book, but a reference tool as well.

FLAGS OF THE AFRICAN PEOPLE $12.95

Copyright 1990

A reference tool for children and adults, outlining flags where people of African heritage are all over the world. This global outlook is provided by following the course of the slave route from Africa to the North, South and Central Americas, the Caribbean, as well as Europe and South Pacific Islands.

KWANZAA — AN AFRICAN CELEBRATION $5.95

Copyright 1991

A simplified manual for observing the Kwanzaa holiday defining the principles and how to arrange the Kinara and other items used during the celebration of the first fruits.

THE CINCO DE MAYO COLORING BOOK $5.95

Copyright 1993

A pictorial history of the Mexican Independence struggle which included African slaves, as well as bi-lingual lessons and captions for each illustration. An effort of collaboration by both African and Hispanic individuals: written by Lady Sala S. Shabazz; translations by Celia Montano Casarez; and, illustrations by Willie Moya.

"Intellectuals ought to study the past not for the pleasure they find in so doing, but to derive lessons from it."

—CHEIKH ANTA DIOP

ORDER FORM

TO ORDER SINGLE COPIES OF "THE BEST OF THE LITTLE KNOWN BLACK HISTORY FACTS", OR 100 COPIES OR MORE FOR YOUR CHURCH, SORORITY, FRATERNITY, OR COMMUNITY ORGANIZATION FUNDRAISER:

☐ PLEASE SEND _________ COPIES OF **THE BEST OF THE LITTLE KNOWN BLACK HISTORY FACTS** AT $14.95 PLUS $3.00 SHIPPING AND HANDLING.

☐ MY ORGANIZATION WOULD LIKE _________ COPIES OF **THE BEST OF THE LITTLE KNOWN BLACK HISTORY FACTS** AT THE DISCOUNT RATE OF $11.00 EACH (MINIMUM ORDER OF 100 COPIES, INCLUDES SHIPPING AND HANDLING.

(Please Print or Type)

NAME: ____

SHIPPING ADDRESS: ____

____

____

NAME OF ORGANIZATION: ____

ADDRESS ____

____

PHONE / FAX NUMBERS ____

AMOUNT ENCLOSED $ ____________

Payment must be included with order by check or money order, payable to: SALA ENTERPRISES.

Mail To:

SALA ENTERPRISES
P.O. BOX 76122
LOS ANGELES, CALIFORNIA 90076

Telephone No.: (213) 957-4900

(Please allow 6 - 8 weeks for delivery)